Resilience on Parade

Short Stories of Suffragists & Women's Battle for the Vote

Jane Hampton Cook

ISBN: 978-0-578-71890-3

Cover Photos
1. Hedwiga Reicher portrays Columbia (the female personification of America) at the Treasury Building, March 3, 1913, for the Washington, D.C., suffrage parade, Library of Congress. 2. Harry T. Burn, in 1918 during his first campaign for Tennessee state representative in McMinn County. Credit T. Boyd 3. Abigail Adams by Benjamin Blythe, Wikimedia Commons 4. Sojourner Truth, 1864 carte de viste, Wikimedia Commons 5. Susan B. Anthony, Wikimedia Commons 6. Inez Milholland, Library of Congress 7. Ida B. Wells by Sallie E. Garrity, Wikimedia Commons 8. Lucy Burns, 1917, Harris & Ewing Collection, Library of Congress 9. Elizabeth Cady Stanton by Napoleon Sarony, National Portrait Gallery Washington 10. Back cover: Suffrage campaign days in New Jersey, August 26, 1915, Library of Congress & Jane Hampton Cook by Jennifer Davis Heffner

Highly recommended!

"Jane Hampton Cook is a consummate researcher, delving into archives and old newspapers to bring events alive in her previous nine historical books. The same thoroughness, scholarly exactness, and lively writing are evidenced in *Resilience on Parade*, her latest effort, and a timely addition to the nation's centennial celebration of women winning the right to vote. Highly recommended!"

—Anthony Pettinato, GenealogyBank.com editor

What a grand way to learn history!

"First, this book is truly greater than the sum of its collected stories. Jane skillfully incorporates quotes that illustrate the era, the beliefs and the contributions to equal rights. Each woman in this book challenges current beliefs and works fervently for change. This is a delightful read that examines not only the history of women's rights, but also the tendency we have to hold onto beliefs even though they may not be valid or may do harm. What a grand way to learn history!"

—Pat Pound, Former Presidential Appointee, National Council on Disability

Resilience on Parade

Short Stories of Suffragists &
Women's Battle for the Vote

Jane Hampton Cook

Wheelhouse Literary
Nashville, TN

Dedicated to my mother
Judy Travis Hampton
(1945-2014)

At the age of four, my mom lost the use of her
shoulder in a polio epidemic but showed resilience
throughout her life as a March of Dimes poster child in
Little Rock, Arkansas (pictured January 28, 1951) and
later as a wife, mother, teacher, and quilter. She paraded
resilience for me each and every day.

CONTENTS

ACKNOWLEDGMENTS

Special thanks to Rebecca Kleefisch, the former Lt. Governor of Wisconsin and former director of the Women's Suffrage Centennial Commission, for her vision for this book and to Jonathan Clements, my longtime literary agent, for his direction and guidance. Thanks also to Alexandra DeSanctis for her editing prowess.

AUTHOR'S NOTE

As I was finishing this book in early 2020, I reflected on these eight remarkable Americans and the qualities that made them special as they battled for women's right to vote. Abigail Adams showed me the importance of taking initiative, while Sojourner Truth demonstrated faith and perseverance.

Yet one quality spoke to me above the rest: resilience. To me, resilience is perseverance on a spring, the ability to bounce back, which I write about in chapters 7 and 8. Within a week of finishing this book, I needed resilience to endure an unexpected cancer workup. Fortunately, the workup showed no cancer, suggesting that the first test was a false positive.

When the COVID-19 pandemic forced Americans to shelter in their homes in March 2020, I realized how much everyone will need resilience to recover from the pandemic's emotional and economic fallout in the days to come.

So, I present to you *Resilience on Parade*. Though these eight Americans represent different qualities, they all showed resilience. Each bounced back from obstacles in their united but elusive goal of women winning the right to vote.

The deep wounds that Elizabeth Cady Stanton and Susan B. Anthony experienced as young women catapulted them on a lifelong quest for justice, one not fully realized in their lifetimes. Lucy Burns and others completed what they had started, tapping into creative courage along the way.

Throughout their lives and especially during a parade, Ida B. Wells-Barnett and Inez Milholland put the two I's in *resilience*, while Harry T. Burn put a dramatic flourish in suffrage's finale. I hope that *Resilience on Parade* will inspire you wherever you are in the parade of life.

Jane Hampton Cook

AMERICA TRIUMPHANT and BRITANNIA in DISTRESS

During America's quest for independence, a weeping Britannia
with a shield (left) and a resilient America (right) are depicted
as women in a Boston almanac, 1782 (Library of Congress).

Columbia, portrayed here in Washington, D.C.'s 1913 women's
suffrage parade. (Treasury Building Library of Congress)

Though America was depicted as a woman named Columbia beginning with the nation's founding, women did not have the universal right to vote until 1920. Columbia was a popular image for World War I posters like this one.
(Library of Congress)

Woman dressed as Columbia, 1917
(Library of Congress)

Margaret Vale, President Woodrow Wilson's niece, New York's
Suffrage Parade, Oct. 1915 (Library of Congress)

The goddess-like Statue of Liberty, c1884 (Library of Congress)

Excerpts from a Poem
about a virtuous goddess representing America

by Phillis Wheatley,
the first published African-American author
October 25, 1775

Celestial choir! enthron'd in realms of light,
Columbia's scenes of glorious toils I write.
While freedom's cause her anxious breast alarms,
She flashes dreadful in refulgent arms.
See mother earth her offspring's fate bemoan,
And nations gaze at scenes before unknown!
See the bright beams of heaven's revolving light
Involved in sorrows and the veil of night!
The goddess comes, she moves divinely fair,
Olive and laurel binds her golden hair:
Wherever shines this native of the skies,
Unnumber'd charms and recent graces rise.
Muse! bow propitious while my pen relates
How pour her armies through a thousand gates:
As when Eolus heaven's fair face deforms,
Enwrapp'd in tempest and a night of storms;
Astonish'd ocean feels the wild uproar,
The refluent surges beat the sounding shore;
Or thick as leaves in Autumn's golden reign,
Such, and so many, moves the warrior's train.
In bright array they seek the work of war,
Where high unfurl'd the ensign waves in air.
Shall I to Washington their praise recite?
Enough thou know'st them in the fields of fight.
Thee, first in place and honours,—we demand
The grace and glory of thy martial band.
Fam'd for thy valour, for thy virtues more,
Hear every tongue thy guardian aid implore! . . .
Fix'd are the eyes of nations on the scales,

For in their hopes Columbia's arm prevails.
Anon Britannia droops the pensive head,
While round increase the rising hills of dead.
Ah! cruel blindness to Columbia's state!
Lament thy thirst of boundless power too late.
Proceed, great chief, with virtue on thy side,
Thy ev'ry action let the goddess guide.
A crown, a mansion, and a throne that shine,
With gold unfading, Washington! be thine.

(Founders.archives.gov)
Wheatley sent this poem to General George Washington,
who loved it so much that he arranged its publication.

Phillis Wheatley, (Library of Congress)

1
INITIATING INDEPENDENCE

What does it mean to take initiative? Is it merely taking a step or something more? When is taking initiative most successful? Is it seizing an opportunity when the conditions are ripe? Captains of sailing ships understood this phenomenon. When the winds were stale or the current was weak, all they could do was move at a slow pace or anchor in place. But when the right wind came, the captain would seize the initiative and set sail.

Abigail Adams grasped this concept, which is why on March 2, 1776, she quoted Shakespeare in a letter to her husband John Adams: "On such a full sea are we now afloat; and we must take the current when it serves, or lose our ventures."[1]

What adventure was Abigail talking about that spring? Though many things were on her mind, two ventures stand out. One was an earth-shaking change. The other was a new code.

John and Abigail Adams found themselves separated in 1775 and 1776. She was living like a single parent, with the full care of their four children in war-torn Massachusetts. Hundreds of miles away in Philadelphia, John was consumed with his new passions—patriotism, public policy, and politics. Despite the

---

[1] Abigail Adams to John Adams, March 2, 1776. See page 188 for this chapter's endnotes.

distance between them, he longed for Abigail, revealing that their separation was physical but not emotional.

"But I never will come here again without you, if I can persuade you to come with me. Whom God has joined together ought not to be put asunder so long with their own consent," he declared to her.

John saw Abigail as his intellectual equal. Though women did not attend school in this era, Abigail had learned to read and write at home as a child growing up in Weymouth, Massachusetts, about twelve miles from Boston. A minister of a church, her father had a large library, which he encouraged Abigail to use.

His library became her dame school, as schooling at home for girls was often called. In New England, the desire for women to be able to read the Bible was very high, and about 90 percent of women learned to read at home, though not all learned to write. As a result of her father's books, Abigail was very knowledgeable, especially about literature and language. John relied on her for her French-speaking skills.

"I wish I understood French as well as you. I would have gone to Canada, if I had. I feel the want of education every day—particularly of that language," he wrote her in February 1776.

Not only that, but he also wanted her to pass along her French skills to their three sons and daughter. "I pray my dear, that you would not suffer your sons or your daughter, ever to feel a similar pain. It is in your power to teach them French, and I every day see more and more that it will become a necessary accomplishment of an American gentleman and lady," he wrote, demonstrating an equality of expectations for both his daughter and his sons.

Adams viewed his wife with great respect and admiration. "I think you shine as a stateswoman, of late as well as a farmeress. Pray where do you get your maxims of state, they are very apropos."

Their relationship and chemistry were built on their mutual

4

intellect. "Nothing has contributed so much to support my mind, as the choice blessing of a wife, whose capacity enabled her to comprehend, and whose pure virtue obliged her to approve the views of her husband," he wrote her.

"This has been the cheering consolation of my heart, in my most solitary, gloomy and disconsolate hours. In this remote situation, I am deprived in a great measure of this comfort. Yet I read, and read again your charming letters, and they serve me, in some faint degree as a substitute for the company and conversation of the writer."

His longing for her during their war-enforced separation led him to write that he wanted to see her think. Yes, watch her think.

"Is there no way for two friendly souls, to converse together, although the bodies are 400 miles off?—Yes by letter.—But I want a better communication. I want to hear you think, or to see your thoughts."

Everything had changed for this Adams and his Eve on April 19, 1775, when the first shots of the American Revolution were fired at the battles of Lexington and Concord outside of Boston. The result was a standoff. Led by General George Washington, the Continental Army surrounded Boston in the countryside, while the British military retreated and occupied the city. The standoff had prevented John from practicing law at his office in town. Hoping to use his leadership skills, he traveled to Philadelphia to serve as a delegate to the Continental Congress. To survive financially, Abigail managed their only other source of income, their farm outside of Boston. While she watched the movements of the Continental Army from her backyard, he debated other members of Congress in Philly.

"I suppose in Congress you think of everything relative to trade and commerce, as well as other things, but as I have been desired to mention to you some things. I shall not omit them," Abigail wrote him on December 10. She was not going to let their separation keep her from speaking up, especially when it came to justice and fairness.

"One is that there may something be done in a continental way with regard to excise upon spirituous liquors that each of the New England colonies may be upon the same footing."

In other words, the people of Massachusetts were paying a tax on liquor when other colonies weren't. She wanted John to use his influence in Congress to correct this imbalance. Because silver wasn't circulating as easily as before, Abigail was also concerned about the devaluation of currency. The result was higher prices for essential goods. Though she was having trouble making ends meet, she was more concerned about the big picture: America's relationship with England. To that end, she'd heard some neighbors complain about Congress.

"I cannot conclude it without telling you, we are all very angry," she explained. Why was she upset? As a member of Congress, John had written some instructions to a New Hampshire assembly on how to run the colony without help from British officials. The result was fear. Despite all of their problems since 1760, when King George III ascended to the throne, especially numerous attempts to tax Britain's American colonies, many colonists were afraid of the winds of change. After listening to their whispers, Abigail realized that too many people weren't ready for what she most wanted for America: declaring independence from England.

"They raise prejudices in the minds of people and serve to create in their minds a terror at a separation from a people wholly unworthy of us," she warned John of the loyalists who were trying to squelch the spirit of independence in New England.

Abigail understood that if a survey were taken in British America in December 1775, not enough people would agree to leave England. Though they were living separately, the Adamses were very much united in a common goal. Both were joined to the idea of independence. They were looking for the right wind for it to set sail. What they found in early 1776 was the gentle

"I have been kept in a continual state of anxiety and expectation ever since you left me. It has been said tomorrow and tomorrow for this month, but when the dreadful tomorrow will be I know not," Abigail expressed her anxiety to John on March 2, 1776, about both his absence and the rumors of a battle that would soon take place in Boston.

As the snow thawed, the countryside was heating up with activity. Both armies, the British in Boston and Washington's troops surrounding it, had ceased fighting for the winter. As spring dawned, she knew that would change.

"But hark! The house this instant shakes with the roar of cannon," she wrote of her lack of sleep and her anxiety that the British would turn her backyard into a battlefield. "I have been to the door and find 'tis a cannonade from our army," she wrote with relief.

"Your distresses, which you have painted in such lively colors, I feel in every line as I read," John replied.

Despite the tension of an impending battle, Abigail had hope that others were coming around to the idea of America separating from England.

"I am charmed with the sentiments of *Common Sense,* and wonder how an honest heart, one who wishes the welfare of their country, and the happiness of posterity can hesitate one moment at adopting them," Abigail wrote about the fast-selling pamphlet that John had recently sent her. Everyone was talking about it. "'Tis highly prized here and carries conviction wherever it is read."

After reading it, she shared *Common Sense* with her neighbors. "I have spread it as much as it lay in my power. Everyone assents to the weighty truths it contains. I wish it could gain credit enough in your assembly to be carried speedily into execution."

What was *Common Sense?* This forty-seven-page pamphlet was

published for the first time in Philadelphia on January 9, 1776, the same day that a ship arrived from England with ominous news. King George III had rejected the peace petition issued by the Continental Congress. Instead, he had declared war against the colonies.

"Perhaps the sentiments contained in the following pages, are not yet sufficiently fashionable to procure them general favor," the anonymous author of *Common Sense* explained. The sure sign that his ideas were resonating and becoming fashionable is that he was unable to keep his pamphlet in print. Within five weeks, the author was printing his third edition.

"It has been very generally propagated through the continent that I wrote this pamphlet," John wrote Abigail. But if he was not the author, then who was?

Born in England thirty-nine years earlier, the author had worked as a sailor, corsetmaker, and school teacher before moving in 1774 to Philadelphia, where he worked as a printer and writer. This man of many trades had come to a conclusion: The English Constitution was sickly. To Thomas Paine, the remedy was a matter of common sense, and he took initiative to write it down and publish it.

The glaring flaw in England's system was that two-thirds of the government was not elected by the people. The king and members of the House of Lords were inherited, unelected positions. As a result, they did not contribute to the freedom of the people. Zeroing in on the king, Paine declared that "absolute power is the natural disease of monarchy."

"There is something exceedingly ridiculous in the composition of monarchy. It first excludes a man from the means of information, yet empowers him to act in cases where the highest judgment is required," he wrote of the people's lack of access to the king. "The state of a king shuts him from the world, yet the business of a king requires him to know it thoroughly." This irony and impossibility made a monarchy absurd and useless.

To Paine, the continuance of this system was the result of

tradition, not common sense. "The prejudice of Englishmen, in favor of their own government, by King, Lords and Commons, arises as much or more from national pride than reason."

He didn't believe that their system was natural or what God had intended. "But there is another and greater distinction for which no truly natural or religious reason can be assigned, and that is the distinction of men into kings and subjects."

Looking at the Old Testament, he analyzed the government under Moses and the Israelites. "Their form of government . . . was a type of republic with a judge and the elders of the tribes. Kings they had none, and it was held sinful to acknowledge any being under that title but the Lord of Hosts." When the people "requested a king," God reluctantly agreed.

What should they do about this problem? "Which is the easiest and most practicable plan, reconciliation or independence?" he asked, stating his radical opinion "that it is the interest of America to be separated from Britain."

To his mind, the most natural reason for political separation was the Atlantic Ocean. It took weeks for a ship to sail from the island of England to the continental shores of North America. "Even the distance at which the Almighty hath placed England and America is a strong and natural proof that the authority of the one over the other was never the design of Heaven."

With the logic of a lawyer and the practicality of a businessman, Paine made his case, leading his readers to this conclusion: "Everything that is right or reasonable pleads for separation. The blood of the slain, the weeping voice of nature cries, 'Tis Time to Part.'"

Making the idea of independence palatable for some and fashionable for many, Paine's logic and practical analysis caught the attention of millions. He published an estimated 500,000 copies, an astounding number considering that the estimated population in the thirteen colonies in 1776 was about 2.5 million people.

For Abigail Adams, *Common Sense* was the remedy she'd been looking for. Its content and popularity led her to conclude that the tide of public sentiment was changing. "I want to know how those sentiments are received in Congress?" she asked in a letter to John. People were now ready to declare independence. "I dare say there would be no difficulty in procuring a vote and instructions from all the assemblies in New England for independency. I most sincerely wish that now in the lucky minuet it might be done."

In her view, the winds were no longer stale. It was time to seize the initiative for the metaphorical ship of independence. "On such a full sea are we now afloat; and we must take the current when it serves, or lose our ventures," she quoted from Shakespeare.

Two days later, on March 4, 1776, Abigail and all of Boston saw a sea change in their military fortunes. General Washington's army posted large cannons on top of Dorchester Heights, which overlooked Boston harbor. This gave his army the upper hand, because they could fire on British supply ships coming in and out of Boston. Within two weeks, on March 17, the British military evacuated the city.

After that, John responded to Abigail's question about what members of Congress thought of *Common Sense*. "You ask, what is thought of *Common Sense?* Sensible men think there are some whims, some sophisms, some artful addresses, too superstitious notions, some keen attempts upon the passions in this pamphlet," he wrote her on March 19.

"But all agree there is a great deal of good sense, delivered in a clear, simple, concise and nervous style. His sentiments of the abilities of America, and of the difficulty of a reconciliation with Great Britain are generally approved. But his notions and plans of Continental government are not much applauded. Indeed this writer has a better hand at pulling down than building."

In other words, Paine had accurately diagnosed the problem and proposed the solution of independence. Less solid to Adams were the specifics of how to build a replacement government.

"This writer seems to have very inadequate ideas of what is

proper and necessary to be done, in order to form constitutions for single colonies, as well as a great model of union for the whole."

Between *Common Sense* and the evacuation of the army, Abigail's spirits had lightened.

"I feel very differently at the approach of spring to what I did a month ago," Abigail wrote John on March 31. She had good news to share about the house they owned in the city of Boston. Though it was dirty, the British doctor had not damaged it during the occupation and evacuation. After giving John an update on the houses of other members of Congress, she shared her optimism.

"We knew not then whether we could plant or sow with safety, whether when we had toiled, we could reap the fruits of our own industry, whether we could rest in our own cottages, or whether we should not be driven from the sea coasts to seek shelter in the wilderness, but now we feel as if we might sit under our own vine and eat the good of the land."

On her mind was the future for John, the Congress, and her beloved country. "I long to hear that you have declared an independency," she wrote on March 31, 1776. She believed that people were ready to seize the initiative and declare independence, but was John convinced?

★ ★ ★ ★ ★

Was the ship of independence ready to set sail? John saw more evidence that the people were ready when he went to church in Philadelphia two months later. "I have this morning heard Mr. Duffield upon the signs of the times. He run a parallel between the case of Israel and that of America, and between the conduct of Pharaoh and that of George," John wrote Abigail on May 14 after hearing Reverend Duffield preach.

"He concluded that the course of events indicated strongly the design of Providence that we should be separated from Great Britain." If ministers were taking the risk of preaching independence from the pulpit, then more and more people were ready. John wondered what his part would be in this unfolding drama. Would he be like Moses, leading the way? Or would he be like Aaron, preparing the way for Moses?

"Is it not a saying of Moses, who am I, that I should go in and out before this great people? When I consider the great events which are passed, and those greater which are rapidly advancing, and that I may have been instrumental of touching some springs, and turning some small wheels, which have had and will have such effects, I feel an awe upon my mind, which is not easily described."

More than ever, John was ready. "Great Britain has at last driven America, to the last step, a complete separation from her, a total absolute independence, not only of her Parliament but of her crown."

The Continental Congress took up the issue of independence in June 1776. Creating a committee to write a declaration, Congress assigned John Adams, Ben Franklin, and Thomas Jefferson to the task. At John's suggestion, Jefferson became Moses, leading the way by writing the declaration. Adams and Franklin served as editors. The Continental Congress adopted the resolution for independence on July 2.

"Yesterday the greatest question was decided, which ever was debated in America, and a greater perhaps, never was or will be decided among men. A resolution was passed without one dissenting colony 'that these united colonies, are, and of right ought to be free and independent states, and as such, they have, and of right ought to have full power to make war, conclude peace, establish commerce, and to do all the other acts and things, which other states may rightfully do,'" John wrote Abigail on July 3.

Up next was debating the Declaration of Independence. "You will see in a few days a declaration setting forth the causes, which have impelled us to this mighty revolution, and the reasons which will justify it, in the sight of God and man. A plan of confederation will be taken up in a few days," he explained. Congress approved the Declaration of Independence on July 4, 1776. A committee set about writing a new constitution, which would ultimately become the Articles of Confederation passed in November 1777.

Though John and Abigail had wanted to see a declaration for independence months earlier, both realized that had they gotten their way, it might have failed. The ship might have wrecked or gone nowhere without the winds of Paine's *Common Sense*.

"Time has been given for the whole people, maturely to consider the great question of Independence and to ripen their judgments, dissipate their fears, and allure their hopes, by discussing it in newspapers and pamphlets, by debating it, in assemblies, conventions, committees of safety and inspection, in town and county meetings, as well as in private conversations, so that the whole people in every colony of the thirteen have now adopted it, as their own act," John wrote Abigail. After sizing up the sentiments of the people, he concluded that seizing the initiative in July 1776 made for a more successful launch of the United States of America. The result was greater unity, because these leaders took initiative under the right circumstances.

"This will cement the union, and avoid those heats and perhaps convulsions which might have been occasioned, by such a declaration six months ago," he wrote.

John predicted that independence would be celebrated by future generations as a day of thanks, with pomp and parades, bonfires, and illuminations.

The most memorable words of the Declaration of Independence are these: "We hold these truths to be self-evident, that all men are created equal, that they are endowed by their Creator with certain unalienable rights that among these are life, liberty and the pursuit of happiness. That to secure these rights, governments are instituted among men, deriving their just powers from the consent of the governed."

Someone who would have recognized these immortal words was John Locke, a philosopher and the son of Puritans in England. Why? He'd written something almost identical to them in 1690. However, had he been alive in 1776, Locke also would have noticed that John Adams, Thomas Jefferson, and Ben Franklin omitted one of his signature words: property.

"Man being born . . . with a title to perfect freedom, and an uncontrolled enjoyment of all the rights and privileges of the law of nature, equally with any other man hath by nature a power, not only to preserve his property, that is, his life, liberty and estate, against the injuries and attempts of other men: but to judge of, and punish the breaches of that law in others, as he is persuaded the offence deserves," Locke had penned in his bestselling work, *Two Treatises of Government*.

Rights are natural, coming from God. The "law of nature gave him for the preservation of himself, and the rest of mankind," Locke explained. All that nature required was for humankind to give some power beneficial for the commonwealth. The commonwealth wasn't a king but a legislative power that "is limited to the public good of the society" with the end goal of preservation. The legislative power can never "have a right to destroy, enslave, or designedly to impoverish the subjects."

Locke's original purpose was to refute the divine right of kings, the philosophy that the king of England was part God and that whatever the king did must be what God wanted. By 1776, both Abigail and John Adams had decided that nothing the king was doing was what God wanted. King George III had become a tyrant. They, along with their generation, were ready to implement Locke's views of the natural rights to life, liberty, and property. Yet when Jefferson replaced the word *property* with the phrase *pursuit of happiness*, he broadened the theory to those who didn't own property. He generalized and equalized the concept, at least in theory.

From Abigail's perspective, there was another word missing from the Declaration of Independence. Though she'd tried to get it included somehow, her failure reveals what happens when the conditions aren't ready for sailing or seizing initiative. The banter that started between a husband and a wife grew into a movement and created a new debate over that missing word.

Abigail Adams, earliest known likeness, at age 24 in 1766
by Benjamin Blyth (Library of Congress).

Abigail Adams, portrait by Gilbert Stuart
(Library of Congress).

2
REMEMBERING THE LADIES

In the lead-up to the Declaration of Independence, Abigail often had taken initiative with John on his behalf and at his request. "I need not tell you, Sir, that the distressed state of this province calls for every excursion of every member of society,"[2] Abigail had written to a London bookseller at the request of her husband shortly after the battles of Lexington and Concord in April 1775. John had wanted her to impress upon this Londoner their situation in the hopes that he would support their cause.

"The spirit that prevails among men of all degrees, all ages and sexes is the spirit of liberty. For this they are determined to risk all their property and their lives nor shrink unnerved before a tyrant's face," she wrote in May 1775.

If the war was affecting every member of society, and each was fighting for liberty, then shouldn't all adults have a say in who represented them? That was Abigail's natural conclusion.

In the months leading to the Declaration of Independence,

---

[2] Abigail Adams to Edward Dilly, March 22, 1775. See page 189 for this chapter's endnotes.

Abigail expressed this view to John in a personal way. Just as she'd passed along the frank opinions of their neighbors and their concerns about the lack of silver and the unfairness of the liquor tax, so she had also shared her views about a matter that meant a great deal to her. Freely giving her opinion on what should guide John and the Congress as they created a new constitution, she also suggested they keep a specific word in mind.

"And by the way in the new code of laws which I suppose it will be necessary for you to make, I desire you would remember the ladies, and be more generous and favorable to them than your ancestors," she wrote John on March 31, 1776.

Abigail didn't hold back.

"Do not put such unlimited power into the hands of the husbands. Remember all men would be tyrants if they could," she continued, underscoring her point with teasing and hyperbole.

"If particular care and attention is not paid to the ladies, we are determined to foment a rebellion, and will not hold ourselves bound by any laws in which we have no voice, or representation."

Though John had frequently addressed her as "my friend" and treated her as an intellectual equal, Abigail knew he was the exception. She didn't hold the same opinion of other men.

"That your sex are naturally tyrannical is a truth so thoroughly established as to admit of no dispute, but such of you as wish to be happy willingly give up the harsh title of master for the more tender and endearing one of friend."

Abigail wanted her husband to protect women from those who didn't respect women the way that he did.

"Why then, not put it out of the power of the vicious and the lawless to use us with cruelty and indignity with impunity. Men of sense in all ages abhor those customs which treat us only as the vassals of your sex," she continued, using the feudal term *vassal* to underscore her point that all men were not uniformly lords over all women.

"Regard us then as beings placed by Providence under your protection and in imitation of the Supreme Being make use of that power only for our happiness," she concluded.

Abigail could trace her interpretation to scripture and John Locke, who had pointed out that "whatever God gave by the words of this grant, Genesis 1:28, it was not to Adam in particular, exclusive of all other men: whatever dominion he had thereby, it was not a private dominion, but a dominion in common with the rest of mankind."

Locke saw mankind as humanity, both male and female. As Locke noted, God didn't give dominion to Adam alone: "For it was spoken in the plural number, God blessed them, and said unto them, have dominion. God says unto Adam and Eve, have dominion."

Locke asked this question about Eve: "Must not she thereby be lady, as well as he lord of the world?" He suggested the dominion of Adam and Eve was mutual. "If it be said, that Eve was subjected to Adam, it seems she was not so subjected to him, as to hinder her dominion over the creatures, or property in them: for shall we say that God ever made a joint grant to two, and one only was to have the benefit of it?"

No, Locke believed. Both male and female were to have dominion. Both had natural rights, which came from God. Abigail obviously agreed. But did her Adam concur? How did he respond?

★ ★ ★ ★ ★

On the surface, John didn't take seriously Abigail's suggestion to remember the ladies. "As to your extraordinary code of laws, I cannot but laugh. We have been told that our struggle has loosened the bands of government everywhere," he wrote her on April 14, 1776, noting that different groups had taken advantage of the lack of government. "But your letter was the first intimation that another tribe more numerous and powerful than all the rest were grown discontented.—This is rather too coarse a compliment but you are so saucy, I won't

20

blot it out."

He tried to soften the blow. "Depend upon it, we know better than to repeal our masculine systems. Although they are in full force, you know they are little more than theory."

Then Mr. Adams tried to turn the tables. "We dare not exert our power in its full latitude. We are obliged to go fair, and softly, and in practice you know we are the subjects. We have only the name of masters, and rather than give up this, which would completely subject us to the despotism of the petticoat, I hope General Washington, and all our brave heroes would fight."

Though Adams didn't appear to take his wife seriously, he in fact did think about it. In May 1776, he engaged in a debate over the question of who had the right to vote in the new government they wanted to build.

In May 1776, Adams read a letter from James Sullivan, a Massachusetts lawyer, who had sent his thoughts about a new code of government to their mutual friend Elbridge Gerry. Sullivan was excited, because leaders in Massachusetts were creating a new legislature. In the lead-up to the Revolutionary War, a British governor had abolished the Charter of Massachusetts Bay Colony and dissolved the legislature. Now it was time to build a new state government.

"A new assembly is at hand in which there will be the most full and equal representation that this colony ever saw. This assembly will undoubtedly suppose it to be their duty to provide for a future less unwieldly and more equal representation than themselves," Sullivan stated, agreeing with *Common Sense* that government should be founded on the people's authority.

"Laws and government are founded on the consent of the people, and that consent should by each member of society be given in proportion to his right," he wrote, believing it was time to think about a new way of giving people a voice. "In order to do it must we not lay aside our old patched and unmeaning form of government?" The way to fix the old government was to ensure that the new one was based on the people's consent.

"Every member of society has a right to give his consent to the laws of the community or he owes no obedience to them," he wrote, noting that this was a true republican principle. But Sullivan saw a huge flaw in the old system.

"And yet a very great number of the people of this colony have at all times been bound by laws to which they never were in a capacity to consent not having estate worth 40/ per annum &c."

What was he talking about? In order to vote in Massachusetts, one had to own land worth forty shillings a year. The result was that only 16 percent of the population was eligible to vote. Of those eligible, only 3.5 percent of the population had voted in the decade before 1774, when the king abolished the Massachusetts government and implemented martial law under a British general. Sullivan saw the contradiction. If only landowners could vote, then more than 80 percent of the people had no voice in choosing their representatives. The resulting system favored the upper class.

Rarely did women own land, much less vote. The rare exception was Lydia Taft of Uxbridge, Massachusetts. When her husband died, she was asked to vote in a town meeting in 1756 during the French and Indian War. Her vote was necessary, because the town needed money from her land to fund the militia. They sought her consent, and she gave it to them.

Lydia Taft lived more than 110 miles from Sullivan, who was born in Berwick, Massachusetts, which is now part of Maine. Nonetheless they shared a common impulse to expand the consent of the governed. Sullivan, who'd recently been appointed to the highest court in Massachusetts in March 1776, was weighing this important principle.

"But yet by fiction of law every man is supposed to consent. Why a man is supposed to consent to the acts of a society of which in this respect he is absolutely an excommunicate, none but a lawyer well dabbled in the feudal system can tell," Sullivan criticized. The current system was blind to this injustice.

Where did this voting structure come from? It originated in the feudal system, in the medieval era of knights and lords. A landlord owned property. His wife, children, servants, and renters, called vassals, all depended on the landlord. The relationship between landlord and vassals was more than just a financial obligation to pay rent once a month. The renter also owed his landlord his service.

Imagine in our modern culture if you rented a house or an apartment. You would pay your landlord a monthly amount in rent and sign an agreement on maintenance for the property. That's it. You wouldn't depend on your landlord for food or a job. If the feudal system were in place, your landlord would also be your boss, giving you instructions and overseeing your work. Your landlord would be your captain in the military, who could order you to the battlefield. Imagine being required to vote the same way your landlord voted. In this structure, the landlord is the only one free and clear of dependency.

"The scars and blotches of the feudal system, the footsteps of vassalage, and the paths to lawless domination compose so great a part of it, that no friend to his country can wish to see it ever put in exercise again," Sullivan wrote, wanting to unshackle his fellow patriots.

Though the medieval era had died out in the 1400s, and many of the obligations between a renter and landlord had disappeared by the 1770s, owning land was still power. In fact, John Locke had used the word "property" 181 times in his *Two Treatises of Government.*

In the 1700s, men and women who did not own land depended on someone who did. Children still depended on women, and women could not go fight because children needed them. Artisans depended on patrons, who were landowners. Renters still depended on landowners for their food and homes. Working-class men, such as blacksmiths, often rented land. All depended on the landlord. They could not vote of their own free will because they had a bias, a debt to a landowner.

The result was that only people who had a free will and were not dependent could vote. Though the words "vassal" and "feudal" weren't in vogue in 1776, the landlord, also called a freeholder, was still the only one in society who was free and clear of dependency. Hence, he could vote freely without obligations to anyone else. In this way, he came to the voting booth independent and unbiased, theoretically not beholden to anyone else's interests.

Excluded from voting were laborers, tenant farmers, unskilled workers, and indentured servants, as well as slaves, women, and children. The result was discrimination and distinctions by class. Some men, in addition to women and minorities, were discriminated against.

Sullivan saw a problem with only landowners voting. He understood the contradiction inherent in declaring that rights come from God and creating a government based on the people when not all people had a say in their consent. The idea that all were equally free and independent contradicted the fact that voting was only available to those who owned land and could vote free and clear of dependency on others. If everyone had to obey the law, shouldn't they have a say in who makes the law?

"For where there is a personal or corporal punishment provided, all subjects are equally concerned—the persons of the beggar, and the prince being equally dear to themselves respectively," he wrote. "Thus, Sir, the poor and rich are alike interested in that important part of government called legislation."

Though rich and poor alike were under the same criminal laws, they differed in the amount of taxes they owed. "But in the supporting the executive parts of civil government by grants and supplies of money, men are interested in proportion to their estates."

How did John Adams respond? He answered Sullivan in a way that showed he'd been thinking about his wife's call to remember the ladies.

"It is certain in theory, that the only moral foundation of government is the consent of the people. But to what an extent shall we carry this principle? Shall we say, that every individual of the community, old and young, male and female, as well as rich and poor, must consent, expressly to every act of legislation? No, you will say. This is impossible," John Adams wrote to Sullivan on May 26, 1776.

John, who didn't own slaves, thought about the 84 percent of society that couldn't vote. "But let us first suppose that the whole community of every age, rank, sex, and condition, has a right to vote. This community is assembled—a motion is made and carried by a majority of one voice. The minority will not agree to this. Whence arises the right of the majority to govern, and the obligation of the minority to obey? From necessity, you will say, because there can be no other rule."

He gave his views on women voting.

"But why exclude women? You will say, because their delicacy renders them unfit for practice and experience, in the great business of life, and the hardy enterprises of war, as well as the arduous cares of state. Besides, their attention is so much engaged with the necessary nurture of their children, that nature has made them fittest for domestic cares."

He explained that children weren't old enough to make decisions and vote before addressing men who didn't own land.

"Is it not equally true, that men in general in every society, who are wholly destitute of property, are also too little acquainted with public affairs to form a right judgment, and too dependent upon other men to have a will of their own?" he asked. "If this is a fact, if you give to every man, who has no property, a vote, will you not make a fine encouraging provision for corruption by your fundamental law?"

He saw non-landowners as a biased special interest loyal to those they depended on. "Such is the frailty of the human heart, that very few men, who have no property, have any judgment of their own. They talk and vote as they are directed by some man of property, who has attached their minds to his interest."

At the root of all of this was fear. Adams feared that the rights of property owners might be overruled by a majority of non–property owners. He understood the problem that non-landowners had to follow the laws.

"Your idea, that those laws, which affect the lives and personal liberty of all, or which inflict corporal punishment, affect those, who are not qualified to vote, as well as those who are, is just. But, so they do women, as well as men, children as well as adults."

"The same reasoning, which will induce you to admit all men, who have no property, to vote, with those who have, for those laws, which affect the person will prove that you ought to admit women and children," he pointed out, acknowledging the logic of opening up the vote to non-landowners.

He viewed men without property in the same way that he viewed women and children. "For generally speaking, women and children, have as good judgment, and as independent minds as those men who are wholly destitute of property: these last being to all intents and purposes as much dependent upon others, who will please to feed, clothe, and employ them, as women are upon their husbands, or children on their parents."

He feared that if Massachusetts gave all men, regardless of class or lack of land ownership, the right to vote, "there will be no end of it. New claims will arise. Women will demand a vote. Lads from 12 to 21 will think their rights not enough attended to, and every man, who has not a farthing, will demand an equal voice with any other in all acts of state. It tends to confound and destroy all distinctions, and prostrate all ranks, to one common level.

"If the multitude is possessed of the balance of real estate, the multitude will have the balance of power, and in that case the multitude will take care of the liberty, virtue, and interest of the multitude in all acts of government," he wrote, believing that it would be wise not to change voting qualifications.

The debate between Adams and Sullivan over who should vote, along with Abigail's cry to remember the ladies, continued in the debate held by the framers of the U.S. Constitution. Meeting in Philadelphia, the members of the Constitutional Convention debated the question of allowing only landowners to vote. Unable to reconcile the issue, they punted.

The framers of the U.S. Constitution in 1787 left the details of who could vote to the states. Article I, section 4 of the Constitution says: "The times, places and manner of holding elections for Senators and Representatives, shall be prescribed in each state by the legislature thereof; but the Congress may at any time by law make or alter such regulations." The Constitution let the states determine who was eligible to vote. Most states kept the status quo by allowing only landowners to vote. In their minds, this was less about discrimination than about unbiased voting.

Despite his opposition to non-landowners voting, John Adams understood the contradiction. He knew that men who owned land had access to education because of their wealth. He understood that owning land carried prestige and opportunity. He closed his debate with Sullivan with a recommendation on solving this disparity.

"Nay I believe we may advance one step farther and affirm that the balance of power in a society, accompanies the balance of property in land," he wrote. His solution was to make more people free of obligations to others by enabling them to become landowners.

"The only possible way then of preserving the balance of power on the side of equal liberty and public virtue, is to make the acquisition of land easy to every member of society: to make a division of the land into small quantities, so that the multitude may be possessed of landed estates."

Abigail Adams couldn't convince her husband to add the

word "women" or "ladies" to either the Declaration of Independence or the Massachusetts Constitution. Though the masses were ready to initiate independence, they weren't ready to initiate equality when it came to voting. Taking initiative succeeds best when there is enough support for the idea. Independence from England could set sail because it was driven by the strong winds of favorability in society. While Abigail's ship of equality faced stale winds, she certainly wasn't alone. Sullivan saw the problem that the Declaration of Independence created by calling for a government based on the consent of the governed while only allowing a small percent of the population, the landowners, the right to vote. With only 3.5 percent of the population actually exercising the vote in the years before the Revolution, the battle to remember the ladies had much to overcome.

Gender is part of our modern definition of diversity. Today we define diversity by gender or sex, race, ethnicity, and class and tend to view the founding era as lacking diversity. But that's not how John Adams saw it.

John and Abigail opposed slavery. He'd supported a passage that Thomas Jefferson wrote for the Declaration of Independence opposing slavery: "The Christian king of Great Britain [is] determined to keep open a market where men should be bought and sold, . . . suppressing every legislative attempt [by the American colonists] to prohibit or to restrain this execrable commerce." Twenty-five percent of Jefferson's original draft was cut, including this passage.

Adams believed there was much diversity in the founding era. In fact, to him, the diversity of the United States made it a miracle that it had come together in the first place. Diversity to Adams was found in religion, primarily the different sects or denominations of Christianity, as well as in Judaism. Defining diversity by religion is a hard concept to grasp in the world today, where all denominations of Protestant and all Catholics are lumped into the category of Christian. But understanding Adams's view of diversity and the challenges it posed puts independence and the lack of universal voting practices into better context.

"But what do we mean by the American Revolution? Do we mean the American war? The revolution was affected before the war commenced," John Adams asked a newspaper editor in 1818.

"The revolution was in the minds and hearts of the people. A change in their religious sentiments of their duties and obligations," he continued, before concluding, "This radical change in the principles, opinions, sentiments and affection of the people, was the real American Revolution."

He saw a difference between Maryland, which was founded by Catholics, and Pennsylvania, which welcomed all religions, from Jews to Quakers. Religion had influenced the different charters of the colonies. "The colonies had grown up under constitutions of government, so different, there was so great a variety of religions, they were composed of so many different nations, their customs, manners and habits had so little resemblance, and . . . their knowledge of each other so imperfect, that to unite them in the same principles in theory and the same system of action was certainly a very difficult enterprise."

The diversity of the colonies wasn't as simple as Christian versus non-Christian but was defined by different sects within Christianity and beliefs about Judeo-Christian theology and values. To John Adams, European Americans were very diverse. A French Catholic was different from an Irish Catholic, and an Irish Catholic was different from an Irish Protestant.

"By what means, this great and important alteration in the religious, moral, political and social character of the people of thirteen colonies, all distinct, unconnected and independent of each other, was begun, pursued and accomplished, it is surely interesting to humanity to investigate, and perpetuate to posterity."

Adams wrote about the real revolution in February 1818. By this time, more men had gained or were gaining the right to vote without owning land. A few months later, in October, Abigail died at the age of 73. She had continued to remember the ladies throughout her life, showing her resilience and her steadfast faith in her beliefs. On one occasion, in 1793, her sister Elizabeth said to her, "I wish you would be so kind as to lend me the *Rights of Women*—the first opportunity." The *Rights of Women* was a book by British author Mary Wollstonecraft, who advocated women's education. Her daughter, Mary Shelley, later gained fame as the author of the novel *Frankenstein.* John had teased Abigail that she was a disciple of Wollstonecraft. And indeed, education for women would pave the path for ladies in the future, enabling them to fight for the right to own land and the right to vote.

The initiative of another Revolutionary War patriot would inspire his granddaughter in the years to come. Descended from the Scottish-Catholic line of Lord Livingston, Colonel James Livingston made a pivotal decision that forever changed American history. While on duty at West Point in 1780, Livingston "took the responsibility of firing into the *Vulture*, a suspicious looking British vessel that lay at anchor near the opposite bank of the Hudson River."

The *Vulture* responded to Livingston's shot by fleeing, leaving a British spy, British major John Andre, behind American lines. "It was a fatal shot for Andre, the British spy, with whom [Benedict] Arnold was then consummating his treason." Livingston had thwarted Andre's escape ship. Andre had been plotting with General Benedict Arnold, who committed treason when he gave Andre the plans to West Point. With the *Vulture* gone, Andre had to walk back to the British lines.

Andre was captured and later executed, but Arnold escaped. Colonel Livingston's granddaughter, Elizabeth, later explained: "On General Washington's return to West Point, he sent for my grandfather and reprimanded him for acting in so important a matter without orders, thereby making himself liable to court-martial." Calming down, Washington "admitted that a most fortunate shot had been sent into the *Vulture*, for . . . the capture of this spy [Andre] has saved us."

Through this event, Livingston passed down a legacy of taking initiative to his granddaughter Elizabeth. The risk Elizabeth later would take would change the tide in the battle to accomplish Abigail's call to remember the ladies.

3
VISION FOR THE VOTE

Elizabeth had every reason to feel on top of the world, both literally and figuratively, as summer dawned in 1840. After all, this twenty-five-year-old New York newlywed was spending her honeymoon in the most luxurious way possible in those days: on a cruise to Europe.

"Fairly at sea, I closed another chapter of my life, and my thoughts turned to what lay in the near future,"[3] she wrote with optimism in her memoirs.

To break the monotony of her eighteen-day journey across the Atlantic Ocean, Elizabeth decided to take a ride up the main mast of the ship *Montreal.* Why shouldn't she? Many a man had done the same thing.

Hoisting herself onto a flat wooden board, she secured her waist with the ropes for safety. Then some sailors pulled the riggings and up she went to the top of the masthead, her toe-length skirt filling up with air like a balloon.

From the top of the main mast, she had a rare aerial view of the *Montreal* and the seemingly endless ocean. To the west behind her unseen was America, her native country. To the east

---

[3] Elizabeth Cady Stanton, *Eighty Years and More*, p. 83. See page 190 for this chapter's endnotes.

in front of her was the soon-to-be visible England, where she and her husband Henry would attend a convention.

Not only could Elizabeth see for miles at the top of that main mast, but she also had a big-picture perspective of the ship below. In the age before air travel, this was truly a rare opportunity. From this aerial spot, she could see the entire deck all at once. In one moment, she had a unique point of view, a vision of what was behind, what was beneath, and what was ahead.

Little did Elizabeth know on that warm summer day that once she reached her destination, she would catch a glimpse of a new vision, one that would become the guiding force of her life and eventually change American history forever. She would do what successful leaders must: create a vision for others to follow.

When she came back down from the thrill at the top of the main mast, she discovered that not everyone was thrilled that she'd taken the ride. Was her new husband, Henry, unhappy? Not at all. Was the ship captain complaining? No. This jolly fellow had planned many diversions for her and encouraged her to explore every nook and cranny of his ship. Who had complained? A politician, and a presidential candidate at that.

Later that night in the ship's saloon, Elizabeth played and won a game of chess against forty-eight-year-old James G. Birney, the Antislavery Party's nominee for president of the United States in the upcoming election. Because an antislavery Kentuckian-turned-New-Yorker was unlikely to win the presidency in 1840, his party had decided to send him as a delegate to the World Anti-Slavery Convention in London instead of campaigning in America.

"Mr. Birney was a polished gentleman of the old school, and was excessively proper and punctilious in manner and conversation," Elizabeth observed, noticing that he frequently criticized others with a goal of improving their manners.

"I soon perceived that he thought I needed considerable toning down before reaching England . . . I was always grateful to anyone who took an interest in my improvement, so I laughingly told him . . . that he need not make his criticisms any longer in that roundabout way, but might take me squarely in hand and polish me up as speedily as possible."

After she beat him at chess that night, she playfully asked for his opinion. "Well, what have I said or done today open to criticism?"

"I heard you call your husband 'Henry' in the presence of strangers, which is not permissible in polite society. You should always say 'Mr. Stanton,'" he added, teasingly noting that she had beaten him in three moves in chess. She could understand his point. Because her husband was serving as a delegate and speaker alongside Mr. Birney at the antislavery conference in London, she needed to meet British etiquette standards.

But that wasn't all. Birney had another criticism.

"You went to the masthead in a chair, which I think very unladylike," he replied in a gracious tone but with clear disapproval.

"Bless me!" Elizabeth facetiously answered. "What a catalogue in one day! I fear my mentor will despair of my ultimate perfection."

"I should have more hope, if you seemed to feel my rebukes more deeply, but you evidently think them of too little consequence to be much disturbed by them," he said.

He was incorrect. She felt a deep sting at his rebuke of her journey up the mainmast. Unladylike? Were only men allowed to ride up the riggings to gain a wider view of their journey? Were women not allowed to enjoy what the ship—or life, for that matter—had to offer?

She long had known the answer to the last question. After all, on more than one occasion, her own father had told her that he wished she had been born a boy.

Fittingly, Elizabeth was born when the men in Johnstown, New York, voted for her father for his only term in Congress.

"I commenced the struggle of life under favorable circumstances on the 12th day of November, 1815, the same year that my father, Daniel Cady, a distinguished lawyer and judge in the state of New York, was elected to Congress," Elizabeth Cady Stanton reflected years later in her memoir, *Eighty Years and More.*

Why did she describe her childhood as a struggle? Elizabeth Cady was born the seventh of ten children. Only five lived a full life. One sister and two brothers had died before she was born, including her brother Daniel, who had been named after her father and had died as an infant the year before her birth. The most memorable of her siblings' deaths took place when Elizabeth was eleven years old.

"My only brother, who had just graduated from Union College, came home to die. A young man of great talent and promise, he was the pride of my father's heart," she reflected when her older brother came home from college at the age of twenty with an illness.

"We early felt that this son filled a larger place in our father's affections and future plans than the five daughters together," she wrote. "Well do I remember how tenderly he watched my brother in his last illness, the sighs and tears he gave vent to as he slowly walked up and down the hall."

Later, in front of her brother's casket, she crawled onto her father's knee and tried to comfort him, but the words that came out of his mouth permanently wounded her soul.

"Oh, my daughter, I wish you were a boy!"

"I will try to be all my brother was," she replied.

From then on, Elizabeth sought to prove her worth to her father by succeeding like a boy. "I thought that the chief thing to be done in order to equal boys was to be learned and courageous. So I decided to study Greek and learn to manage a horse."

No matter how hard she studied, how well she did in school, how skilled she became at leaping fences on a horse, how many prizes she won defeating boys in the mastery of Greek, nothing softened her father's disappointment that she was a girl.

"I taxed power, hoping someday to hear my father say: 'Well, a girl is as good as a boy, after all.' But he never said it." Instead, after she shared an achievement of hers with him, her father would say, "Ah, you should have been a boy!" Her joy often was turned to sadness.

Another way that Elizabeth tried to gain her father's admiration was to spend time in his law office, which was attached to their family home. There she listened to her father's clients, talked with the law students studying under him, and read laws, especially those applying to women.

"In our Scotch neighborhood many men still retained the old feudal ideas of women and property. Fathers, at their death, would will the bulk of their property to the eldest son, with the proviso that the mother was to have a home with him," she reflected.

"Hence it was not unusual for the mother, who had brought all the property into the family, to be made an unhappy dependent on the bounty of an uncongenial daughter-in-law and a dissipated son."

Elizabeth watched many widows plead their cases and beg her father for a way to retain ownership of their property. "The tears and complaints of the women who came to my father for legal advice touched my heart and early drew my attention to the injustice and cruelty of the laws." Seeing their plight tore at her sense of justice and led her to question her father's response.

"As the practice of the law was my father's business, I could not exactly understand why he could not alleviate the sufferings of these women. So, in order to enlighten me, he would take down his books and show me the inexorable statutes."

Soon his law students turned her interest in laws affecting women into a game. "The students, observing my interest, would amuse themselves by reading to me all the worst laws they could find, over which I would laugh and cry by turns." Sometimes they went too far.

"One Christmas morning I went into the office to show them, among my other presents, a new coral necklace and bracelets. They all admired the jewelry and then began to tease me with hypothetical cases of future ownership."

One of them suggested that he could take her necklace from her. "Now, if in due time you should be my wife, those ornaments would be mine; I could take them and lock them up, and you could never wear them except with my permission. I could even exchange them for a box of cigars, and you could watch them evaporate in smoke."

The law students also teased her by reading excerpts from British classics, such as Shakespeare's *Taming of the Shrew,* and other works that suggested the headship of men over all women. Elizabeth disagreed with their interpretation: "My mind never yielded to this popular heresy."

All of this was too much taunting for her taste. "With this constant bantering from students and the sad complaints of the women, my mind was sorely perplexed."

Then she had an idea. Enraged about these laws and frustrated at being teased, she threatened to cut all of the statutes against women out of her father's law books. "Becoming more and more convinced of the necessity of taking some active measures against these unjust provisions, I resolved to seize the first opportunity, when alone in the office, to cut every one of them out of the books; supposing my father and his library were the beginning and the end of the law."

Getting word of her plan, her father intervened and explained to her how laws were made. Cutting them out of his law books wouldn't change them. Only the New York legislature could change state laws. Only Congress could change the federal ones.

"When you are grown up, and able to prepare a speech, you must go down to Albany and talk to the legislators; tell them all you have seen in this office—the sufferings of these Scotch women, robbed of their inheritance and left dependent on their unworthy sons, and, if you can persuade them to pass new laws, the old ones will be a dead letter."

In that moment, he planted a vision of activism in her mind. Maybe she could do something to change the injustice she felt personally and witnessed through her father's widowed clients. These wounds would become the kindling on a fire that would fuel her success as a visionary leader.

Fortunately, Elizabeth's interactions with boys her own age were a contrast to the older law students and her father. Unlike in Abigail Adams's day, Elizabeth's generation of women were allowed to attend school up to a point.

Elizabeth felt she was an equal with the boys at Johnstown Academy. "Though I was the only girl in the higher classes of mathematics and the languages, yet, in our plays, all the girls and boys mingled freely together. In running races, sliding downhill, and snowballing, we made no distinction of sex."

Graduation, however, ended her sense of freedom and harmony with boys. Her male classmates went to Union College at Schenectady, while she was forced to attend an all-girls finishing school, a seminary. "When those with whom I had studied and contended for prizes for five years came to bid me good-by, and I learned of the barrier that prevented me from following in their footsteps—'no girls admitted here'—my vexation and mortification knew no bounds."

Her bitterness grew worse at the all-girls school. "Again I felt more keenly than ever the humiliation of the distinctions made on the ground of sex."

Then came Henry Stanton. Mistakenly believing that he was engaged, she relaxed and felt free to be herself when she met him at her cousin's house. "Mr. Stanton was then in his prime, a fine-looking, affable young man, with remarkable conversational talent, and was ten years my senior, with the advantage that that number of years necessarily gives." She was smitten the first time she heard him give a speech. "As I had a passion for oratory, I was deeply impressed with his power."

They shared a sense of justice and desire for social reform, particularly abolishing slavery. "I had become interested in the antislavery and temperance questions, and was deeply impressed with the appeals and arguments." The temperance movement was an effort to root out alcoholism. Henry was "the most eloquent and impassioned orator on the antislavery platform."

Traveling with him on speaking tours of New York, she was soon ready to become Mrs. Stanton. "I shall never forget those charming drives over the hills in Madison County, the bright autumnal days, and the bewitching moonlight nights," she wrote of their budding romance. "It seemed to me that I never had so much happiness crowded into one short month."

For the first time, she had a vision for her life that was hopeful. "I felt a new inspiration in life and was enthused with new ideas of individual rights and the basic principles of government, for the antislavery platform was the best school the American people ever had on which to learn republican principles and ethics."

Though her cousin warned her that her father, who'd previously owned slaves, would never consent to her marrying an abolitionist, she had her way. Henry and Elizabeth married in early May 1840 in Johnstown and embarked on their cruise to England that same month as Mr. and Mrs. Stanton.

★ ★ ★ ★ ★

While traveling on that ship to England, Elizabeth was determined to thoroughly understand the abolitionist movement in America. She wanted to be prepared to discuss the issue with the delegates to the World Anti-Slavery Convention in London.

Before they arrived in Europe, Elizabeth seized an opportunity to put Mr. Birney in his place. She had seen him, more than once, ridicule some of the ship's British working-class passengers. One day she asked him a question, one that sprung from the sting she'd felt over his reprimand for going up the mainmast in a chair.

"Is it good breeding to make fun of the foibles of our fellow-men, who have not had our advantages of culture and education?" she asked solemnly. He got her point.

"He felt the rebuke and blushed, and never again returned to that subject. I am sorry to say I was glad to find him once in fault."

Elizabeth, Henry, and Mr. Birney arrived in London and stayed at the same hotel as the other Americans, including several female delegates such as Quaker preacher Lucretia Mott, who'd traveled on a separate ship. They were among more than 500 attendees to the World Anti-Slavery Convention, which began on June 12, 1840.

That same day, *The Liberator,* an abolitionist newspaper in Massachusetts, predicted that the convention would be controversial. Why? Though the delegates were united in opposition to human slavery, they were divided over another issue: women.

"I think the convention will be a stormy one . . . If the meeting is free, all will be peace. If a woman is allowed to be gagged there, the moral hurricane will be awakened," *The Liberator* editorialized. The British organizers had expressed their opposition to women serving as delegates, which allowed them to speak. The issue had caused a split among Anti-Slavery Society members in America. Mr. Birney opposed women delegates. The editor of *The Liberator* supported them for many reasons, including this one: The current monarch of England was a queen.

"If Victoria can be Lord High Admiral of England, the head of her navies and grand marshal of her forces by land as well as head of the church, Lucretia Mott may bear testimony against human slavery in England in a peaceful, quiet convention of Christians," *The Liberator* wrote on the day the convention opened.

How did Henry feel about the issue? He'd joined Mr. Birney in opposing women delegates during the dustup leading to the convention. But by the time of the convention, he'd listened to Elizabeth. "My husband made a very eloquent speech in favor of admitting the women delegates," she wrote.

The attendees of the World Anti-Slavery Convention debated women's participation for an entire day. Elizabeth was astonished at the irony. "It struck me as very remarkable that abolitionists, who felt so keenly the wrongs of the slave, should be so oblivious to the equal wrongs of their own mothers, wives, and sisters, when, according to the common law, both classes occupied a similar legal status," she reflected.

While Elizabeth wasn't a delegate, several American women were. "Though women were members of the National Antislavery Society, accustomed to speak and vote in all its conventions, and to take an equally active part with men in the whole antislavery struggle, and were there as delegates from associations of men and women, as well as those distinctively of their own sex, yet all alike were rejected because they were women."

The result was silence. Elizabeth, Lucretia, and the American women delegates and British female observers were forced to listen in silence while men gave speeches for the purpose of the convention: opposing slavery.

"Judging from my own feelings, the women on both sides of the Atlantic must have been humiliated and chagrined," she wrote, noting that the women sat in a section hidden by a curtain as if they were church choir.

One of the male delegates, William Lloyd Garrison, refused to participate because women couldn't. "After battling so many long years for the liberties of African slaves, I can take no part in a convention that strikes down the most sacred rights of all women," Garrison declared. The division revealed a complicating factor of social reform in the 1800s. Internal disagreements often divided organizations and took their focus away from reforming the injustice that united them.

Mr. Birney became so frustrated listening to the American women discuss the issue over meals during the convention that he changed hotels. "Having strongly opposed the admission of women as delegates to the convention it was rather embarrassing to meet them, during the intervals between the various sessions, at the table and in the drawing room," he wrote.

The discrimination against women at this convention opened the door for new friendships for Elizabeth. For the first time, she met other women who viewed equality of the sexes the same way that she did. She spent some time with forty-seven-year-old Lucretia Mott, and described her by writing, "She had not much faith in the sincerity of abolitionists who, while eloquently defending the natural rights of slaves, denied freedom of speech to one-half the people of their own race."

Why did the British oppose letting women participate in the convention? They interpreted the fall of Adam and Eve to mean that all women were subservient to all men. Elizabeth shared Lucretia's interpretation of Genesis, which was similar to Abigail Adams's interpretation and John Locke's view. "Male and female created he them, and blessed them, and called their name Adam," Mott often explained.

"He gave dominion to both over the lower animals, but not to one over the other . . . The cause of the subjection of woman to man, was early ascribed to disobedience to the command of God," Mott said.

For Elizabeth, the World Anti-Slavery Convention's discrimination against women was a game-changer, especially emotionally. For the first time in her life, she had received what her father never gave her—validation in her belief that women were created equal and had equal value and worth.

"The acquaintance of Lucretia Mott, who was a broad, liberal thinker on politics, religion, and all questions of reform, opened to me a new world of thought. As we walked about to see the sights of London, I embraced every opportunity to talk with her," Elizabeth reflected. "It was intensely gratifying to hear all that, through years of doubt, I had dimly thought, so freely discussed by other women, some of them no older than myself—women, too, of rare intelligence, cultivation, and refinement."

Then Mott, who was twenty years older than Stanton,

planted a vision in her protégé. "As Mrs. Mott and I walked home, arm in arm, commenting on the incidents of the day, we resolved to hold a convention as soon as we returned home, and form a society to advocate the rights of women."

Other women held the same hope. "As the convention adjourned, the remark was heard on all sides, 'It is about time some demand was made for new liberties for women.'" The injustice Elizabeth witnessed gave rise to a new generation of leaders. "The action of this convention was the topic of discussion, in public and private, for a long time, and stung many women into new thought and action and gave rise to the movement for women's political equality both in England and the United States."

How long would it take for the seeds of equality to grow and take root? Part of her vision would come to life within a decade. The other would not happen in her lifetime.

Eight years after the World Anti-Slavery Convention, Elizabeth Cady Stanton had become a desperate housewife.

"Then, too, the novelty of housekeeping had passed away, and much that was once attractive in domestic life was now irksome," she reflected on her life as a wife and mother in 1848. "Up to this time life had glided by with comparative ease, but now the real struggle was upon me."

Elizabeth and Henry had loved living in Boston, where they'd mingled in the large circle of social reformers. Unlike her mother and father, she and her husband hadn't faced the tragedy of losing a child at a young age. However, Boston's colder climate became too much for Henry. In 1847, they moved their family of three sons to Seneca Falls, New York.

"The house we were to occupy had been closed for some years and needed many repairs, and the grounds, comprising five acres, were overgrown with weeds," she reflected. In other words, they had bought a fixer-upper. "My father gave me a check and said, with a smile, 'You believe in woman's capacity to do and dare; now go ahead and put your place in order.'"

Elizabeth got to work purchasing timber, brick, and paint, which introduced her to Ansel Bascom, who helped her repair her house. He was a member of New York's constitutional convention that was meeting in Albany at the time.

"I urged him to propose an amendment to Article II, Section 3, of the State Constitution, striking out the word 'male,' which limits the suffrage to men. But, while he fully agreed with all I had to say on the political equality of women, he had not the courage to make himself the laughing-stock of the convention," she reflected.

In the early 1800s, state constitutions expanded the right to vote from landowners to working-class men but did not include men who were paupers. Property qualifications were replaced by tax-paying qualifications. In order to do this, some states had placed the word "male" in the laws and constitutions. The result was more-definitive discrimination against women.

In New Jersey, women who owned property were allowed to vote from 1776 until 1807. When too many women were voting for the Federalist Party, leaders of the Democratic-Republican Party inserted the word "male" into New Jersey's suffragist laws to take votes from Federalists, and property-owning women in New Jersey lost the right to vote.

While trying to obtain the right for women to vote in her home state of New York, Elizabeth also worked unsuccessfully on a bill to protect married women's property rights. A good negotiator, she'd intervened with a neighbor whose alcoholic husband had beaten her. These challenges fueled her blues.

"My duties were too numerous and varied, and none sufficiently exhilarating or intellectual to bring into play my higher faculties. I suffered with mental hunger, which, like an empty stomach, is very depressing."

Her desperation reached a peak in the summer of 1848. "My experience at the World's Antislavery Convention, all I had read of the legal status of women, and the oppression I saw everywhere, together swept across my soul, intensified now by many personal experiences. It seemed as if all the elements had conspired to impel me to some onward step."

She knew the source of her desperation, which gave her a vision for change. "The general discontent I felt with woman's portion as wife, mother, housekeeper, physician, and spiritual guide . . . and the wearied, anxious look of the majority of women impressed me with a strong feeling that some active measures should be taken to remedy the wrongs of society in general, and of women in particular."

A quote by Ralph Waldo Emerson encouraged her: "A healthy discontent is the first step to progress." Her mind returned to the idea of a women's convention. "I could not see what to do or where to begin—my only thought was a public meeting for protest and discussion."

She wasn't alone. In July 1848, Lucretia Mott returned from spending a month at the Seneca tribe's farm and school in New York. The Senecas were discussing the need to reorganize their government. Not only that, but the Seneca women were also taking part in the debate. They had a vote. Freshly inspired by the suffrage of the Seneca sisters, Mott gathered some like-minded friends to spend the day with her. Elizabeth seized the opportunity.

"There I met several members of different families of friends, earnest, thoughtful women. I poured out, that day, the torrent of my long-accumulating discontent, with such vehemence and indignation that I stirred myself, as well as the rest of the party, to do and dare anything."

A vision is meaningless if a leader lacks the passion to carry it through. The sisters of Seneca Falls were ready to step up and lead. Meeting on July 13, 1848, the five women—Elizabeth Cady Stanton, Lucretia Mott, Mary Ann McClintock, Jane Hunt, and Martha C. Wright—decided to take action. "My discontent, according to Emerson, must have been healthy, for it moved us all to prompt action, and we decided, then and there, to call a Woman's Rights Convention," Cady Stanton wrote?

They sent an invitation to the *Seneca County Courier,* which published the announcement for the convention, which met five days later on July 19-20. Then they got to work on the convention's agenda. They needed something that women could fight for, but what could that possibly be?

"The convention, which was held two days in the Methodist Church, was in every way a grand success. The house was crowded at every session, the speaking good, and a religious earnestness dignified all the proceedings," Elizabeth reflected of the 300 people who attended the convention, including Ansel Bascom, the man she'd lobbied to redefine male suffrage in New York's constitution.

Elizabeth found herself on the top of the world during the Seneca Falls women's convention on July 19 and July 20, 1848. "These were the hasty initiative steps of 'the most momentous reform that had yet been launched on the world—the first organized protest against the injustice which had brooded for ages over the character and destiny of one-half the race.'"

Just as she'd seen the big picture from the top of the *Montreal*'s masthead in 1840, so she and the other ladies presented an aerial view of the past, present, and future for women at Wesleyan Chapel in Seneca Falls through the Declaration of Sentiments. Antislavery groups had used the same approach by issuing and publicizing a declaration of sentiments against slavery.

The Seneca Falls Declaration of Sentiments looked back and took inspiration from the past, specifically the Declaration of Independence. Declaring that women's rights came from God, they used language similar to that of Thomas Jefferson:

"When, in the course of human events, it becomes necessary for one portion of the family of man to assume among the people of the earth a position different from that which they have hitherto occupied, but one to which the laws of nature and of nature's God entitle them, a decent respect to the opinions of mankind requires that they should declare the causes that impel them to such a course."

They applied the Declaration's most famous line to females. "We hold these truths to be self-evident; that all men and women are created equal; that they are endowed by their Creator with certain inalienable rights; that among these are life, liberty, and the pursuit of happiness; that to secure these rights governments are instituted, deriving their just powers from the consent of the governed."

With these words, they didn't degrade America's founding or try to tear it down and start over. Rather, they applied the founding's principles to women, remembering them and taking initiative as Abigail Adams had.

They didn't hold back as they looked back. "The history of mankind is a history of repeated injuries and usurpations on the part of man toward woman, having in direct object the establishment of an absolute tyranny over her. To prove this, let facts be submitted to a candid world."

Their present goal was "to demand the equal station to which they are entitled." Topping the list of "usurpations on the part of man toward woman" was denying women the right to vote. "He has never permitted her to exercise her inalienable right to the elective franchise." The result was that women were expected to obey laws "in the formation of which she had no voice."

When it came to the right vote, the first generation of Americans under the Constitution had broken with the British system by abolishing the monarchy. The early decades led to the uneducated working class of freemen gaining the right to vote. Even the most "ignorant and degraded men" had the right to vote. Despite the discrimination by race and gender, the American suffrage system was groundbreaking by the mid 1800s compared to the suffrage system in Great Britain.

At that time in England, only 2 to 3 percent of the population—highly wealthy men—had the right to vote. In England, only 20 percent of the population owned land and could vote in 1700, which dwindled to 17.2 percent in 1754 and

12 percent by 1820. By contrast, working men who didn't own land in America had gained the right to vote.

"Having deprived her of this first right of a citizen, the elective franchise, thereby leaving her without representation in the halls of legislation, he has oppressed her on all sides," the declaration stated.

Their vision was for women to vote. After all, if women could vote, they could hold legislators accountable. They could change laws. They could establish justice. Women's suffrage would become the guiding force—the premier vision—of all else. No matter the generation, leaders need a just vision to inspire and guide them.

Despite a noble vision, the present reality was harsh. "He has made her, if married, in the eye of the law, civilly dead." Their sentiments focused on the rights of women, both married and single, in the areas of property, wages, education, employment, and divorce.

"He has monopolized nearly all the profitable employments, and from those she is permitted to follow, she receives but a scanty remuneration. He closes against her all the avenues to wealth and distinction, which he considers most honorable to himself. As a teacher of theology, medicine, or law, she is not known."

The sentiments focused on the state as well as the church, noting cultural obstacles against women, especially a lack of education. "He has denied her the facilities for obtaining a thorough education—all colleges being closed against her."

Striking at society's double standards for men and women, they declared, "He has created a false public sentiment, by giving to the world a different code of morals for men and women, by which moral delinquencies which exclude women from society, are not only tolerated but deemed of little account in man."

The sentiments accused the generic male of taking God's place. "He has usurped the prerogative of Jehovah himself, claiming it as his right to assign for her a sphere of action, when that belongs to her conscience and her God."

They ended by claiming that women were U.S. citizens, a declaration that later would be questioned in the wake of the end of slavery. "Now, in view of this entire disfranchisement of one-half the people of this country, their social and religious degradation—in view of the unjust laws above mentioned, and because women do feel themselves aggrieved, oppressed, and fraudulently deprived of their most sacred rights, we insist that they have immediate admission to all the rights and privileges which belong to them as citizens of these United States."

One-hundred people signed their Declaration of Sentiments, including sixty-eight women and thirty-two men. How were the convention and the sentiments received by the public?

The *Vermont Mercury* printed excerpts of the sentiments saying, "Hear, O man, with what thou art charged by these female Hancocks and Jeffersons . . . the signers to this document, about a hundred are not to be sneezed at." What was the *Vermont Mercury*'s recommendation? Ignore these women and their convention.

The Declaration of Independence had identified twenty-five abuses of King George III. The ladies had replaced the king's name with *he,* referring to men generally. This technique made it hard for many men to accept the statements. It was one thing to impugn the King of England, an invisible being across the ocean, and make him the enemy. It was another to impugn a generic male, which risked offending every father, husband, and son—the very voters who could elect the legislators that women needed to make changes to laws that discriminated against them.

"The women in arms," Ossining, New York's *Westchester Herald* wrote of this rebellion against those in trousers. "It is evident the age of chivalry is no more," the paper wrote, predicting that remorseless tyrants would be left with taking care of babies and households.

After printing the sentiments, the editor of Brattleboro, Vermont's *Semiweekly Eagle* responded satirically: "It seems that this is not a free country after all, but no one will deny that it is a great country."

Elizabeth was pained by the criticism. "No words could express our astonishment on finding, a few days afterward, that what seemed to us so timely, so rational, and so sacred, should be a subject for sarcasm and ridicule to the entire press of the nation," she reflected. "With our Declaration of Rights and resolutions for a text, it seemed as if every man who could wield a pen prepared a homily on 'woman's sphere.'"

"All the journals from Maine to Texas seemed to strive with each other to see which could make our movement appear the most ridiculous. The antislavery papers stood by us manfully and so did Frederick Douglass, both in the convention and in his paper, *The North Star*, but so pronounced was the popular voice against us, in the parlor, press, and pulpit, that most of the ladies who had attended the convention and signed the declaration, one by one, withdrew their names and influence and joined our persecutors."

Despite the blowback, the women at Seneca Falls had a plan for implementing their vision. Knowing they would face ridicule and misunderstanding, they vowed to spread their vision in the press, in pamphlets and tracts. In doing so, they wanted to target all levels of government. Their strategy was to hold a series of conventions.

"Our friends gave us the cold shoulder and felt themselves disgraced by the whole proceeding," Elizabeth reflected.

While she felt the sting of rejection, Elizabeth had a reason to celebrate at this time. The property bill for married women passed in New York. Elizabeth had spoken before the committee. "The same year of the convention, the Married Woman's Property Bill, which had given rise to some discussion on woman's rights in New York, had passed the legislature," she reflected, noting that this had encouraged more activity.

"Hence the demands made in the convention were not entirely new to the reading and thinking public of New York—the first state to take any action on the question. As New York was the first state to put the word 'male' in her constitution in 1778, it was fitting that she should be first in more liberal legislation," she continued.

"The effect of the convention on my own mind was most salutary. The discussions had cleared my ideas as to the primal steps to be taken for woman's enfranchisement, and the opportunity of expressing myself fully and freely on a subject I felt so deeply about was a great relief," she wrote.

"I think all women who attended the convention felt better for the statement of their wrongs, believing that the first step had been taken to right them."

The first step was the vision, the idea of giving women the right to vote and correcting the laws that discriminated against them. Success would be a long slog and would require another one of life's secrets. One woman's personal story of perseverance combined the abolitionist movement with the women's rights movement, culminating in a memorable speech.

Elizabeth Cady Stanton holding her daughter Harriot (left)
and many years later (right) (Library of Congress).

Elizabeth Cady Stanton and Susan B. Anthony
(Wikimedia Commons).

4
PERSEVERING TRUTH & FAITH

The old preacher had just one more thing to do before she died and met the Great Emancipator in heaven. After a lifetime of persevering through many trials, she had to meet the Great Emancipator on Earth.

Isabella's parents had told her the story so often she was sure she had seen it with her own eyes. Deep inside, however, she knew the truth. She was only an infant when it had happened, but the incident was tattooed on her heart as deeply as the scars lashed on her back.

Mau-mau, her mother, always described it best. Her five-year-old brother arose when the birds began to sing that winter morning in 1787. Because it was snowing outside, the little boy dutifully got up from his place on the floor next to his three-year-old sister. He tiptoed across the boards, careful not to splash mud on the faces of those who were still sleeping. He'd made the others mad many times before by being too loud in the morning. Though they slept in the master's cellar, the boards were so loose and the floor so full of dirt they might as well have been sleeping in the barn. Then her brother kindled a fire in the fireplace. Soon they'd be warm, or at least less cold than they were.

Baby Isabella lived with her two older siblings and their parents. Because slaves were not allowed to legally marry, her mother and father were husband and wife only in the eyes of God, not the law. If they had been a white family, they would have been known by a last name, but they didn't have a family name. Her father was called Bomefree, a slang Dutch name meaning "tree." The reason for his name was as simple as it was obvious. He was tall and straight like a tree.

They were some of several slaves owned by Charles Ardinburgh of Ulster County, New York. By day, Ardinburgh's slaves raised tobacco, corn, and flax. By night, they slept in the cellar, the basement of his hotel. Their numbers varied, depending on how many he could afford at one time. One thing was certain: No matter how many slaves he owned or their gender, they all slept in the cellar. With a little straw for pillows, they slept like horses on the floor.

That particular morning, after awakening from his place on the floor, Isabella's brother called for his Mau-mau to tell her the fire was ready. Not long after that, he heard the sound of horses.

With great curiosity, the little boy stretched his arms as high as he could. He jumped and grabbed the window sill. Then he pulled himself up, just enough to glance through the room's only window, before jumping down with a thud and splashing mud on his legs.

"A large, old-fashioned sleigh, was seen to drive up to the door,"[4] Isabella reflected in her memoirs. But when she heard the news, Mau-mau felt a familiar pain, the kind that went from her heart into her stomach, wrenching from within. She had seen the sleigh before.

"This event was noticed with childish pleasure by the

---

[4] Sojourner Truth, *Narrative of Sojourner Truth*. See page 193 for this chapter's endnotes.

unsuspicious boy." But Mau-mau knew what it meant. She stretched out her arms to hug her little boy, but he wiggled away, darting again toward the window. He was too excited to be still for a long embrace.

Within minutes, the driver came into the cellar. He told the boy he had a surprise for him. He was taking him in a sleigh ride over the snow. Oblivious to the anguish in his mother's face, the little boy raced past the man and ran up the stairs. He freely jumped into the sleigh, excited about the ride ahead. He had ridden in an old wagon before but never in a smooth sleigh over the snow.

The driver soon appeared, but he was not alone. He carried the boy's three-year-old sister, whose screams boomeranged to the moon and back. She was also going on the sleigh ride. Then the driver opened up a crate at the back of the sleigh, put the girl inside, and shut the lid to silence her screams.

Seeing his sister caged, the little boy's glee turned to horror. With the speed of a frightened deer, he ran back inside the house and hid under a bed. But the driver was strong and pulled him out with little trouble. He was "separated forever from those whom God had constituted his natural guardians and protectors." No matter the screams muffled by the closed crate, the deal was done. Mau-mau listened as the sleigh drove away. Though she didn't know where they were going, she knew one thing for sure. She would never see them again.

Whenever he needed money, Master Ardinburgh sold one of Mau-mau and Bomefree's children, as if they were nothing more than cattle. To him, that's what they were, animals to be bought and sold to another owner without regard for Providence's plan for parents to care for their children. Of the ten children she had born, only her baby Isabella remained—for the moment.

As she grew, Isabella often found her mother crying.

"Mau-mau, what makes you cry?" she asked in Low Dutch.

The answer was always the same: "Oh, my child, I'm thinking of your brothers and sisters that have been sold away from me."

Then Mau-mau would tell the tales, recalling the moment when each of her children had been taken away. The memories crucified her heart over and over. But as often as Mau-mau passed down those terrible tales, she gave Isabella hope. Despite all of their struggles and the injustice her family faced during this time, her mother demonstrated faith. She passed along a belief in God to Isabella. Her mother knew that she had a window of time to teach Isabella. The likelihood of her being taken away like her siblings was high.

Not only did her mother encourage her to have faith in God, but she also lived by example. She taught Isabella at a young age to pray using the Lord's Prayer.

From her mother, Isabella learned to persevere in truth. Her father Bomefree may have been named for an upright tree, but Mau-mau was the figurative pillar of the family. She was a pillar of prayer, a rod of faith, an example that Isabella never forgot, especially during her darkest days.

The iron sticks lashed her back for the last time. It was over. Her whipping was done.

Nine-year-old Isabella had been whipped before, but this was the worst she'd ever received. The day was Sunday. She had received a lashing on the Lord's Day, but she knew it wasn't with the Lord's blessing.

Her new mistress had told her to go to the barn. When Isabella arrived she saw him, her new master, standing there. In his hands was a bundle of poles, which had been heated in the embers of a fire and tied together with cords. She trembled like a deer staring at the barrel of a rifle.

He bound her, tying her hands and removing her clothes. Then he whipped her bare flesh, over and over again. She screamed throughout the torture.

He whipped her until the lacerations on her back were deep and more numerous than the roots of a tree. Blood streamed from her wounds. The beating was so severe she would bear the scars for the rest of her life.

By this time, Isabella had suffered the same fate as her older siblings. She didn't remember much about the auction, only that she had been sold for one-hundred dollars, along with some sheep that shared her sojourn to Ulster County. Her new master and new mistress, Mr. and Mrs. Nealy, didn't seem too bad at first.

"Now the war began," she later recalled of her conflict with them.

The problem was simple. The Nealys only spoke English. Isabella only spoke a form of Dutch, often called low or slang Dutch. She had a difficult time knowing what they needed. Once they asked her to fetch a frying pan. Not understanding, she brought them hooks for the pots. Torture taught her English.

As she lay lifeless and bleeding in the barn after her beating that Sunday, she knew exactly what she needed to do, but she would have to wait until after sunset. As soon as darkness fell over the earth, Isabella went outside. She stared at the glittering stars and the bright moon. She hoped God could see such a little girl under such a big rich sky.

She remembered how her Mau-mau would sit down with her and tell her about God. Often they sat outside under the stars, heaven's sparkling blanket, as her mother called it.

"My children, there is a God, who hears and sees you," Mau-mau had often said.

"A God, Mau-mau! Where does he live?" Isabella had asked just as often.

"He lives in the sky," she answered. "And when you are beaten or cruelly treated, or fall into any trouble, you must ask help of him. He will always hear and help you."

Remembering her mother's words, Isabella told God that she hadn't lied or stolen anything. Her Mau-mau had taught her to be honest. Though she'd lived up to this, she promised God she would act just right. She told him she was sorry she hadn't thought to ask for his help before the beating.

She remembered something else. She asked God the same question she had heard her mother repeat as many times as there are stars in that sky.

"Oh Lord, how long?" Isabella shouted as loudly as she could.

Her shouting wasn't disrespectful. She just wanted to make sure God could hear her as her mother had taught her. She had to keep going, to persevere.

"Those are the same stars, and that is the same moon, that look down upon your brothers and sisters, and which they see as they look up to them, though they are ever so far away from us, and each other," Mau-mau had said.

As Isabella stared at the sky, she could take comfort that her Mau-mau might have been staring at the sky at same time. How long it would be before she would see her Mau-mau again? Would she be a mother someday? If so, would her children be sold away, too?

As this tiny girl faced such tall thoughts, she endured the stinging of her wound. Was the oozing sweat or blood? Her whole body ached. But under the starts, she felt free to pray the Lord's Prayer as her mother had taught her. Her new master may not have understood her Dutch, but God did.

★ ★ ★ ★ ★

"How can I get away?" Isabella thought, fearing that the answer was as elusive as the water rushing through the stream surrounding her tiny little island.

"God, I'm afraid to go in the night, and in the day, everybody would see her," she contemplated.

Once again, Isabella had taken refuge in her outdoor prayer room. She believed that if she presented her requests to God under the open sky then he would hear her, especially if she spoke very loudly. She chose some rocks that stood out in the middle of a stream. Shielding the rocks were willow trees, whose limbs bent and swayed easily. Although they appeared to be limp, the willows were symbols of her faith, pillars of prayer kneeling before God. Joining her were sheep, who found the spot a place of refuge from the hot sun, the same animals with which she'd been sold years earlier.

By this time, Isabella was grown, nearly thirty-years-old. She was tree-like, tall and erect like her father. Although she never saw her mother again, she had been allowed to go to her funeral. Isabella had been sold to a few masters over the years, but she had lived with Master Dumont for a long time. Now she had five children of her own. All but her infant had been sold away from her. Though she was in love with someone else, she had been forced to marry another man. Now he was gone too, sold away with sheep or pigs, whichever fetched the better price.

Isabella's decision to leave was not because Dumont had treated her poorly. He wasn't cruel to her, but he had broken a promise to her. When the state of New York declared that all slaves would be emancipated on July 4, 1828, Dumont had promised Isabella she could be free a year earlier, on July 4, 1827. He gave her only one condition: She must work hard. For weeks, Isabella had worked harder than at any other time in her life. She had spun about one-hundred pounds of wool. When a new sickness in her hand caused her great pain and slowed her progress, Dumont reneged. She wouldn't let him get away with it. She responded with faith.

From that island protected by the willow trees, Isabella prayed her most daring thought. The noise of the rushing water concealed her shouting. She knew it was time to escape. As she prayed about getting away, an idea struck her mind with the force of a thunderbolt.

"Yes," said she, fervently. "That's a good thought. Thank you, God, for that thought."

Then she left her wee willow-tree island, hoping it was for the last time.

The next day, a little before daybreak, with her infant on one arm and a cotton handkerchief containing two articles of clothing and some modest provisions, she struck out from Master Dumont's home. The time of day was from God, the thought he had placed in her mind under the willows. When she reached the summit of a high hill, quite a distance from Dumont's house, she had another thought, one she hadn't considered before.

Where would she go? And to whom?

She stopped to feed her infant and prayed to God for direction. No sooner had she prayed than she remembered something. A man she knew lived in the direction she was heading. Sure enough, not long after she resumed her walk, she arrived at his house.

His relatives greeted her warmly. When they learned her plight, they knew exactly where she should go: to the Van Wageners, a Dutch family. After she traveled to their house, they warmly took her in and employed her.

Not long after she had been with the Van Wageners, Mr. Dumont arrived.

"Why, Bell, so you've run away from me," he said with surprise in his voice when he saw her.

"No, I did not run away. I walked away, by daylight, and all because you had promised me a year of my time."

"You must go back with me."

He persisted, using guilt as his carrot, but Isabella refused to be treated like a horse.

"No, I won't go back with you."

"Well, I shall take the child."

Her answer was the same.

At this point, Mr. Van Wagener intervened. Although he didn't believe in slavery, he offered to buy her services for the remaining balance of the year. Van Wagener paid twenty dollars for Isabella and five dollars for her child. Then, in front of Dumont, Van Wagener gave Isabella a very important instruction. She was not to call him master but rather address him as *Mr. Van Wagener*. This Dutchman would not be a master to anyone.

"There is but one master; and he who is your master is my master," Van Wagener proclaimed, revealing his Quaker faith.

Dumont left, never bothering Isabella again. She broke with custom for emancipated slaves and took the last name of Van Wagener, not the name of her last master, Dumont. Through the influence of the Quakers, her faith grew. Through them, she learned God was all-knowing. He knew her thoughts. She realized that she didn't have to speak loudly to be heard by the Almighty anymore.

But her faith had yet to meet its greatest challenge. This trial would test her perseverance beyond any circumstance she had ever known.

As soon as Mr. Van Wagener told her the news, she knew what she must do. Although she dreaded going to that place, she had no choice. The life of one of her children, a son, was at stake.

Determination led Isabella to the house of Mr. Gedney. Shortly before she had earned her freedom, Mr. Dumont, her old master, had sold her five-year-old son to Dr. Gedney, who promised to take the boy no farther than New York City. Instead Dr. Gedney sold him to his brother, Solomon Gedney, who sold him to their sister's husband, a wealthy planter named Fowler who lived in Alabama. Mr. Van Wagener explained to Isabella that the law prohibited the sale of any slave out of state. The act was even more odious to him because the boy had been sold to the South, where slavery remained legal.

When she arrived at the Gedney home, she immediately called upon Mrs. Gedney, the mother-in-law of her son's new master.

"Dear me! What a disturbance to make about your child. What? Is your child better than my child?" she sneered, referring to her daughter, Eliza Fowler, who was the boy's new mistress living in Alabama. Mrs. Gedney used a racial slur, the oral equivalent to a thousand lashes.

"I'll have my child again!" Isabella shouted.

"Have your child again?" the woman replied scornfully.

"How can you get him? And what have you to support him with, if you could?"

"No," answered Isabella. "I have no money but God has enough, or what's better! And I'll have my child again."

Then Mrs. Gedney laughed as if a demon lived inside her.

As she walked back to the Van Wagener's house, she was sure she'd have her son again. The Van Wageners had told her about someone. His name was Jesus. She had heard of Jesus and figured that he was special, like George Washington or General Lafayette. She was mistaken. Through the Van Wageners, she learned that Jesus was God's son, the Savior. He was her intercessor, the Great Emancipator in heaven. It was in him she was determined to believe. It was to him that she turned in her great hour of need.

"I was sure God would help me to get him. I felt so tall within. I felt as if the power of a nation was with me."

Through prayer and persistence, Isabella took her case to court. An officer of the court instructed her on how to make a lawful oath. She swore on the Bible that the child she spoke of was her son. The judge issued papers. They served Solomon Gedney with the unlawful sale of the boy. Failure to bring him back from Alabama would result in fourteen years in prison and a $1,000 fine.

While she waited, she prayed and told others of her determination to have her son again.

Isabella hurried to the house of the judge, where the lawyer told her to go to claim her son. When she saw him, her heart leaped so high she could have jumped over an acre of willow trees. Her son was alive. The best news was that he was also out of the South. As she rushed to him, the child pushed her away, clinging to Solomon Gedney.

Through his cries, he denied that he'd ever seen her before.

He claimed he didn't have a mother. At first his reaction shocked and wounded her, but she had not forgotten what it was like to be under the spell of a master, or, rather, under the spell of a whipping.

The judge continued to question the boy and asked him how he got the scar on his forehead.

"Fowler's horse hove him gave it to me," he said of being thrown from a horse. What about the one on his cheek?

"That was done by running against the carriage," the boy said, looking away from the judge. He clutched his master's leg even more tightly, hiding his face from Isabella, and assured them that Fowler had been kind to him. Tears streamed from his face.

The judge turned to Isabella and asked if she could swear this was her son.

"Yes, I swear it's my son."

She was certain the man had threatened her little boy so he wouldn't tell the truth. She knew her son was not really denying her. He was simply scared. Isabella's attorney pleaded her case, explaining the boy's illegal sale. She held her breath while the judge proclaimed his decision. It was the "sentence of the court for the boy to be delivered into the hands of his mother—having no other master, no other controller, no other conductor but his mother."

The boy was given to her. After receiving assurance that his master would not be able to take him back, he stopped crying.

"Well, you do look like my mother used to," he said to Isabella.

Then he told her of how his master had beaten him.

"Oh, Jesus, look! See my poor child. Oh, Lord, 'render unto them double' for all of this!" she cried.

Not long after this, Isabella heard some terrible news. Fowler, the boy's former master, had murdered his wife, the daughter of Mrs. Gedney. Isabella felt guilty for praying for double against them. Although the incident was horrible, she knew what many former slaves knew about cruel masters.

Those who ignored the humanity of slaves and equated them with cattle would soon treat their family members or neighbors without regard for life.

Isabella couldn't help what other people did. All she could do was make sure the two children under her care had a safe place to sleep and food to eat.

★ ★ ★ ★ ★

The fifty-four-year-old black woman, who often wore a turban woven with brightly colored threads, entered the convention in Akron, Ohio, that spring day in May 1851. Isabella Van Wagener no longer existed.

When she left Dumont's house of bondage, she left everything behind. Years later, she went to the Lord and asked Him to give her a new name after her conversion to Christianity in 1848. The Lord gave her Sojourner, because she was to travel up and down the land to show the people the sin of slavery and to be a sign unto them. Later, she wanted a last name, because everyone had two names, and God gave her Truth because she was to proclaim truth to the people.

As the attendees of the women's rights conference in Akron on May 29, 1851, would soon discover, Sojourner Truth may have entered that conference known as an abolitionist, but she left it known by another name, too—suffragist.

"May I say a few words? I want to say a few words about this matter," she began, saying that she was an example of women's rights.

"I have as much muscle as any man, and can do as much work as any man. I have plowed and reaped and husked and chopped and mowed, and can any man do more than that?" Indeed, as her autobiography declared, she'd endured the toil of slavery and had the lashes to prove it.

"I have heard much about the sexes being equal; I can carry as much as any man, and can eat as much too, if I can get it. I am as strong as any man that is now.

"As for intellect, all I can say is, if women have a pint and man a quart - why can't she have her little pint full?" Her pint had recently been full. This woman who could not read had become a published author the previous year. How was that possible?

She'd shared with abolitionist Oliver Gilbert her story of perseverance and how she'd transformed from a slave into a free person, and he had written it down and published it. Called *Narrative of Sojourner Truth* by Sojourner Truth, her story shed light on the cruelties of slavery and launched her into the role of an activist. It was time to stand up for African women.

"You need not be afraid to give us our rights for fear we will take too much, for we can't take more than our pint'll hold. The poor men seem to be all in confusion, and don't know what to do," she continued.

"Why children, if you have woman's rights, give it to her and you will feel better. You will have your own rights, and they won't be so much trouble," she said in her own version of remember the ladies.

"I can't read, but I can hear. I have heard the Bible and have learned that Eve caused man to sin. Well if woman upset the world, do give her a chance to set it right side up again," Sojourner proclaimed, turning her talk into a mini sermon of sorts.

"The lady has spoken about Jesus, how he never spurned woman from him, and she was right. When Lazarus died, Mary and Martha came to him with faith and love and besought him to raise their brother. And Jesus wept—and Lazarus came forth. And how came Jesus into the world? Through God who created him and woman who bore him."

Then she ended with a zinger, recognizing the dual reform movements facing the nation: abolition and women's rights. She represented both.

"Man, where is your part? But the women are coming up blessed be God and a few of the men are coming up with them. But man is in a tight place, the poor slave is on him, woman is coming on him, and he is surely between-a hawk and a buzzard."

The most memorable speech of that convention, her remarks as presented here were published a few weeks after her speech by Marius Robinson in the *Anti-Slavery Bugle* of New Lisbon, Ohio, on June 21, 1851. The event's organizer, Frances Dana Gage, published another version in 1863 in the *New York Independent*. Hailed by suffragists, it was branded as *Ar'n't I a Woman?* The accuracy of Gage's version is doubtful because it was published twelve years after she first delivered it. Regardless, the speech brought Sojourner notoriety.

Around this time, Sojourner traveled to Massachusetts, where she met Harriet Beecher Stowe, whose book *Uncle Tom's Cabin* was the *Common Sense* of the Civil War. Harriet wrote about their meeting in the *Atlanta Monthly*.

Sojourner believed that if God could help her do such big things as speaking at the women's conference or meeting Harriet Beecher Stowe, then he would help her meet the man she most wanted to meet in the world. Heaven's Great Emancipator would help her meet the emancipator of her people.

In October 1864, Truth's ultimate sojourn led her to the great white house where he lived. As she stared at the pillars flanking the president's house, her mind may have flashed back to the island of the willow trees, her kneeling pillars of prayer under the stars above. She had never seen such a grand house before, whose columns reached to the sky as if to proclaim something special, such as justice or freedom. Then she walked into the house as freely as anyone else.

A dozen or so guests waited in the president's reception area. Sojourner noticed that two of the women were also black. A gentleman escorted the guests one by one to the president, who was seated in an adjacent room. One observation made her smile.

He showed as much kindness and consideration to the colored persons as to the whites, in her opinion. It was hard to hold back a tear or two. If there was any difference, he showed more pleasantries to the emancipated. Then her moment came. The gentlemen escorted her to the president's desk.

"This is Sojourner Truth, who has come all the way from Michigan to see you," the host said, introducing her to the president.

Abraham Lincoln stood, extending his hand to her. She responded by taking his hand and shaking it. Then he bowed.

"I am pleased to see you," he said.

As many people did before meeting a president, she had rehearsed a thousand times what she planned to say.

"Mr. President, when you first took your seat I feared you would be torn to pieces, for I likened you unto Daniel, who was thrown into the lions' den. And if the lions did not tear you into pieces, I knew that it would be God that had saved you; and I said if He spared me I would see you before the four years expired, and He has done so, and now I am here to see you for myself."

Tapping his wit, Lincoln congratulated her on being spared.

"I appreciate you, for you are the best president who has ever taken the seat."

Lincoln paused, perhaps crossing his long arms as if thinking.

"I expect you have reference to my having emancipated the slaves in my proclamation," he said, naming many of his predecessors, especially Washington. "They were all just as good, and would have done just as I have done if the time had come," he said, pausing again.

"If the people over the river," he said, pointing across the Potomac, "had behaved themselves, I could not have done which gave me the opportunity to do these things."

"I thank God that you were the instrument selected by Him and the people to do it," Sojourner replied, acknowledging that she hadn't heard of him before he became president. He upped the compliment, noting that he'd heard of her many times before.

Lincoln then turned toward his desk, sat down, and picked up a large elegant book. He told her it had been given to him by the colored people of Baltimore.

Sojourner was speechless as she stared at the Bible. She glanced at the president. He nodded, as if giving her permission to open it and look through it.

"This is beautiful indeed; the colored people have given this to the head of the government, and that government once sanctioned laws that would not permit its people to learn enough to enable them to read this book. And for what? Let them answer who can."

Then Sojourner pulled a small book from her skirt pocket and handed it to the president.

He picked up a pen from his desk and wrote, "For Aunty Sojourner Truth, Oct. 29, 1864. A. Lincoln."

Lincoln stood and took her hand with his large bony hand, the same one that had signed the Emancipation Proclamation. He told her he would be pleased to have her call upon him again.

Sojourner smiled. As she exited through the door and passed through the pillars of the president's house, she wanted to shout to God and thank him for Abraham Lincoln, but she didn't have to shout to be heard by the Almighty anymore. God knew her heart.

"I felt that I was in the presence of a friend, and I now thank God from the bottom of my heart that I always have advocated his cause, and have done it openly and boldly. I shall feel still more in duty bound to do so in time to come. May God assist me."

Now more than ever, she would advocate for her people, her now free people. She longed to return home, to make Michigan a place where the emancipated could come and pursue life, liberty, and happiness. Perhaps one day she could vote. As she began her journey home, she believed that the Greatest Emancipator would help her.

Sojourner's story of perseverance shows leaders the value of taking the next step, of the will to keep going, of the strength to push through the worst hardships, and of faith in their vision no matter what. Leaders sometimes face difficult choices. The suffrage movement was no different. One teacher would soon learn how and when to change strategies and tactics while keeping her eye on the big picture.

Sojourner Truth & Abraham Lincoln
(Library of Congress)

Isabella Bomefree, who became
Sojourner Truth (Library of Congress)

5
CALCULATING STRATEGIES

The two mathematical problems staring at this teacher were unjust. How could a math equation render a verdict? The multiplication problems she'd calculated were unjust for one reason. They were unequal. How could she possibly balance the equations? She didn't know it at the time, but she'd spend a lifetime trying, doing what visionary leaders must often do. She tapped different strategies and tactics to try to reach her goal.

"Her experience as a school teacher, her compensation being but $8 a month, while men received for the same service from $24 to $30"[5] a month, the press relayed of the math problems that had dogged her. "After fifteen years of the closest economy, she had only saved $300 out of her meager salary, while, had she received equal compensation for equal service, her savings would have aggregated at least $2,000."

This teacher had calculated that if she were a male, her salary and savings would have been three to six times higher. "This contrast aroused her conceptions of injustice."

---

[5] *Daily Illinois State Register,* March 30, 1884. See page 194 for this chapter's endnotes.

Beginning to teach by age sixteen, Susan Brownwell Anthony was born in 1820 into a family that valued education. When her father, Daniel Anthony, moved his brood to New York's Hudson Valley region, he divided his home into living quarters, his store, and his children's schoolroom. There Susan and her five siblings were taught by various teachers. Some of them were women.

Wanting to further her education, her father sent her to Deborah Moulson's Female Seminary, which was a Quaker boarding school in Philadelphia. The financial panic of 1837, however, sent her family into poverty and forced them to sell everything they owned. They also moved a couple of times, eventually landing in Rochester, New York. This left Susan with little choice but to leave the female seminary and work to pay off her father's debts. She became a teacher, rising to headmistress of the female department of Canajoharie Academy in Rochester.

This is where her math calculations of inequality began. As part of her teaching duties, Susan B. Anthony attended the New York Teacher's Convention in Rochester. Despite the fact that women outnumbered men ten to one at the convention, women didn't give speeches or participate in discussions. That didn't stop Susan. "Although a member on equal footing with others, she caused a sensation by rising to speak to the question, 'Why the profession of teacher was not as much respected as that of minister, lawyer or doctor,'" an Anthony biographer wrote in *Woman Suffrage and Politics.*

Raised a Quaker, Susan knew that women were allowed to speak at Quaker meetings. "Where do you, find a nobler type of womanhood than in the Quaker Church, where woman is required as spiritual teacher, equal with man?" she later described.

Her father's Quaker faith instilled in her a belief of equality, regardless of race, sex, or class. She saw no reason that a convention of educators should be different.

"At length President Davis of West Point, in full dress, buff vest, blue coat, gilt buttons, stepped to the front and said in tremulous mocking tone 'What will the lady have?'"

"I wish, Sir, to speak to the question under discussion," she answered. A gentleman moved that she be heard, which was seconded. After debating for half an hour whether she could speak, a small majority finally agreed to allow it.

"Do you not see, gentlemen, that so long as society says a woman is incompetent to be a lawyer, minister, or doctor, but has ample ability to be a teacher, that every man of you who chooses this profession tacitly acknowledges that he has no more brains than a woman?" Needless to say, her comment wasn't well-received.

However, a newspaper reporter thought that she accurately captured the reason teachers weren't as well respected as other professions. It was one of the few professions, despite its pay inequities, that women could join. The next morning's *Rochester Democrat* reported: "Whatever the schoolmasters may think of Miss Anthony, it is evident that she hit the nail on the head."

What did Susan learn from that experience? Plenty. Despite the equation of inequality that this convention gave her, she would soon become a leader who understood the strategic value of educating the public through the social media of her generation.

"The annual national convention for the advancement of women's rights assembled yesterday morning," New York's *Evening Post* relayed on October 19, 1854, of a major event taking place in Philadelphia. "And attracted a collection of several hundred females, mostly Friends, with a sprinkling of males," the news reported of the prevalence of Quakers, also called the Society of Friends, in attendance. Another newspaper noticed that the convention was better attended the following day "and we noticed quite a number of distinguished gentlemen present."

The convention made a fashion statement. "Miss (Lucy) Stone being in Bloomer costume, was the observed of all observers; from the neatness of her attire, and the grace with which it was worn did much to commend it to public approval." Bloomers were ballooned pants worn under ankle-length or shorter dresses. Named after Amelia Bloomer, who wrote about them in her magazine, they allowed for freer, safer movement. Unlike the teachers' convention, most of the speakers were women.

"Mrs. Susan B. Anthony, of Rochester, made a speech, in which she detailed the steps taken by the women of New York, and the progress made in petitioning the legislature of that state," the press reported, incorrectly identifying her as a married woman. Another report noted that she also called for donations.

By this time, Susan had left the teaching profession. Instead, she had decided to become an activist. At first, her two primary causes were the abolitionist movement, which sought to eliminate slavery, and the temperance movement, which sought to abolish alcohol. She joined the Daughters of Temperance in Canajoharie in 1848 and then became its presiding sister. She became the principal New York agent for the American Anti-Slavery Society in 1856. One particular abolitionist meeting a few years earlier in 1851 in Seneca Falls, New York, stood out because it changed her life. Why? There she met Elizabeth Cady Stanton.

Becoming instant friends, the pair worked side-by-side in their multiple mutual activist causes. Together they founded the Women's New York State Temperance Society in 1852 and helped to organize the Whole World's Temperance Convention a year later. Elizabeth, however, convinced Susan that voting was the conduit to all of the other social changes she sought, such as equality of salaries and empowering women who were married to alcoholics.

"She labored as sincerely in the temperance movement, until convinced that woman's moral power amounted to little as a civil agent until backed by ballot and coined into state law," Elizabeth later reflected on Susan.

Though united in the common vision of women's rights and women's suffrage, they had to develop a strategy to achieve their goal. Conferences were the social media of their day. People would meet to discuss and debate issues. These gatherings allowed people to network, organize, and come together for a common cause. From Susan's point of view, conferences were the perfect strategy. As a former teacher, she knew how to educate. Conferences were a tactical way to implement the strategy of educating the public. Deciding to broaden their local conferences, Anthony and Stanton were key players, along with Lucretia Mott and Lucy Stone, in hosting annual national women's rights conferences.

"From 1852, she has been one of the leading spirits in every women's rights convention held in America," the press relayed of Susan's contribution.

One of the resolutions from the 1854 national women's rights conference combined Susan and Elizabeth's life experiences. "That so long as woman is debarred from an equal education, restricted in her employment, denied the right of independent property if married, and denied in all cases the right in controlling the legislation which she is nevertheless bound to obey, so long must the woman's rights agitation be continued.

"Resolved that in perfect confidence that what we desire will one day be accomplished, we commit the cause of woman to God and to humanity."

They chose different tactics to accomplish their strategy. Elizabeth, whose maternal responsibilities made it difficult for her to travel, wrote speeches that Susan delivered. Elizabeth was the faster, better writer, gifted with rhetoric, while Susan was excellent with numbers and facts. She was also quite good at critiquing and editing. Theirs was a balanced, efficient working relationship. While Stanton often "forged the thunderbolts," Anthony "fired them."

Within four years, Susan presided over the annual conference. They saw positive reforms, such as laws that allowed women to own property, control their wages, and retain custody of their children after divorce. But no matter how effective their strategy and tactics, a circumstance beyond their control forced change. The Civil War ended their annual conferences. While Anthony wanted to continue them, Stanton and others didn't think it was appropriate to hold them while the nation was at war. Who won? Not Susan. The conferences stopped for a few years.

Though the Civil War had stalled the women's rights movement, Anthony and Stanton supported the war effort. When President Lincoln sought a mandate to emancipate the slaves, the ladies responded with resilience and renewed vigor.

Calculating the need for a new approach, they created a new organization, called the Woman's National Loyal League, which met in New York City on May 14, 1863. Their tactics were an equation of addition by combining abolishing slavery with women's suffrage. They hoped equality for all would be the result.

"'Governments derive their just powers from the consent of the governed.' This is the fundamental principle of democracy," Susan proclaimed. "The political and civil rights of every citizen must be practically established. . . . It is not because women suffer. It is not because slaves suffer. . . . it is the simple assertion of the great fundamental truth of democracy that was proclaimed by our Revolutionary fathers.'"

The calculation coming from the Women's National Loyal League couldn't have pleased Susan more. Anthony and Stanton got to work. They collected thousands of signatures on petitions calling for slavery's end. One of their most loyal women's suffrage supporters, Senator Charles Sumner, presented their first installment of 100,000 signatures calling for the abolition of slavery.

"I offer a petition now lying on the desk before me. It is too bulky for me to take up. I need not add that it is too bulky for any of the pages of this body to carry," he noted. The addition of 200,000 more signatures supplied President Lincoln's mandate and set the foundation for the Thirteenth Amendment to the Constitution that abolished slavery. The petitions cemented the loyalty of women's suffragists, or so they thought. All seemed well, until Susan encountered another unjust multiplication problem.

The math staring at Susan in 1865 as she read a newspaper article stunned her as much as it pained her, deeply. While visiting her brother in Leavenworth, Kansas, she came across an article about a new proposed amendment to the Constitution. She saw something she'd never seen before in the U.S. Constitution or in one of its proposed amendments. What was it? The word "male." Staring at her in a draft of the Fourteenth Amendment was the word "male," not once, not twice, but three times. The first section of the draft gave anyone born in the United States citizenship, which would make former slaves U.S. citizens. She agreed with this. The second section, however, included a lengthy paragraph that greatly concerned her because of how it would affect women.

"But when the, right to vote at any election for the choice of electors for President and Vice-President of the United States, Representatives in Congress, the Executive and Judicial officers of a State, or the members of the Legislature thereof, is denied to any of the *male* inhabitants of such State, being twenty-one years of age, and citizens of the United States, or in any way abridged, except for participation in rebellion, or other crime, the basis of representation therein shall be reduced in the proportion which the number of such *male* citizens shall bear to the whole number of *male* citizens twenty-one years of age in such State." [Emphases added.]

Susan feared that inserting the word "male" into the Constitution for the first time would disenfranchise all women, regardless of race, and degrade them to a lower political status than they currently held. It would make it even harder to give women the right to vote. Racing home to New York, she contacted former suffrage supporters. She soon realized that the zeal she'd seen from many before the war had tapered off. She calculated that she could revive the issue by holding meetings, visiting towns, and asking for support. Her petition drive caught lawmakers' attention.

"When Congress convened on December 4, (1865) petitions were already arriving, protesting against the introduction into the constitution of the word *male*. Few Senators or Representatives escaped a bombardment of letters and petitions urging that the nation should take no such backward step as to write the word *male* into the Constitution."

But that wasn't all in their strategic arsenal. Sometimes leaders must contemplate a merger or take stock of their environment. The suffragists put a fresh twist on their old strategy. They held a national women's rights conference in May 1866 and announced a new organization, the American Equal Rights Association. Knowing that many in Congress had frowned on their petitions opposing the word "male" in the Fourteenth Amendment, they calculated that a game of addition might be in their favor. They asked that all women, regardless of their race, have the right to vote.

"The ballot for women, white and black, the crowning right of civilization," the *New York Herald* declared of their goal. They sent a resolution to Congress and asked that women's suffrage become a priority. Anthony gave a speech.

"Men and parties, must pass away, but justice is eternal; and they only who work in harmony with its laws are immortal. All who have carefully noted the proceedings of this Congress, and contrasted your speeches with those made under the old régime of slavery, must have seen the added power and eloquence that greater freedom gives. But still you propose no action on your grand ideas," Susan declared to the conference, taking a big-picture perspective.

"Your joint resolutions, your reconstruction reports do not reflect your highest thought. The Constitution in basing representation on 'respective numbers' covers a broader ground than any you have yet proposed," she continued, referring to the drafted Fourteenth Amendment. "But the only tenable, ground of representation is universal suffrage, as it is only through universal suffrage that the principle of 'Equal Rights to All' can be realized."

She reminded Congress of the support that women suffragists gave to abolishing slavery and supporting the Civil War. "With you we have just passed through the agony of death, the resurrection and triumph of another revolution, doing all in our power to mitigate its horrors and gild its glories. And now think you, we have no souls to fire, no brains to weigh your arguments; that after education such as this, we can stand as silent witnesses while you sell our birthright of liberty?" she chided. "Our demand must ever be: 'No compromise of human rights. No admission in the constitution of inequality of rights, or disfranchisement on account of color or sex.'"

They sent a copy of their resolution to every member of Congress. Despite their efforts, Congress passed the Fourteenth Amendment with the word "male" and without the word "female" on June 13, 1866.

Part of the equation they now faced was a matter of measuring time. The American Equal Rights Association started brightly, with hope. Henry Ward Beecher, the brother of author Harriet Beecher Stowe, presented a memorable analogy about the opportunities this post-war time offered them.

"I am not a farmer, but I know that the spring comes but once a year. When the furrow is open is the time to put in your seed if you would gather a harvest in its season. Now, when the red-hot plowshare of war has opened a furrow in this nation, is the time to put in the seed. If any man says to me 'Why will you agitate the woman question, when it is the hour for the black man?' I answer, it is the hour for every man, black or white," he said, believing that the public mind was open.

"Don't wait until, the public mind shuts up altogether. Progress goes by periods, by jumps and spurts. We are in the favored hour. I, therefore, say whatever truth is to be known for the next fifty years in this nation let it be spoken now," he said, hoping that the time was ripe to strike for all.

"I propose that you take expediency out of the way, and that you put a principle that is more enduring than expediency in the place of it—manhood and womanhood suffrage for all. You may just as well meet it now as at any other time. You never will have so favorable an occasion, so sympathetic a heart, never a public reason so willing to be convinced, as today."

Susan B. Anthony and Elizabeth Stanton were also eloquent. "We believe that: humanity is one in all those intellectual, moral and spiritual attributes out of which grow human responsibilities. The Scripture declaration is, 'So God created man in his own image, male and female created he them,' and all divine legislation throughout the realm of nature recognizes the perfect equality of the two conditions; for male and female are but different conditions," Anthony and Stanton wrote. "Neither color nor sex is ever discharged from obedience to law, natural or moral, written or unwritten. The commandments thou shalt not steal, or kill, or commit adultery, recognize no sex.

"Women and colored men are loyal, liberty-loving citizens, and we cannot believe that sex or complexion should be any ground for civil or political degradation. Against such outrage on the very name of a republic we do and ever must protest; and is not our protest against this tyranny of 'taxation without representation' as just as that thundered from Bunker Hill, when our Revolutionary fathers fired the shot which shook the world?

"We respectfully and earnestly pray that, in restoring the foundations of our nationality, all discriminations on account of sex or race may be removed; and that our government may be republican in fact as well as form; A government by the people, and the whole people, for the people and the whole people." Susan also became the corresponding secretary of the American Equal Rights Association.

But eloquence and strategy were not equal to two factors working against them: politics plus expediency.

Not all mergers work. When the American Equal Rights Association held its first anniversary in New York in 1867, a tense debate erupted over the proposed Fifteenth Amendment to the Constitution. The proposal planned to give freedmen, but not women, the right to vote.

They passed this resolution: "Resolved that as both the Republican and Democratic parties, in limiting the right of suffrage and establishing an oligarchy of sex and race are false to the theory of our government, we urge upon the people everywhere to organize a new party on the basis of equal suffrage to all men and women and holding the balance of power between the two old parties, say to these compromise of human rights 'come up higher.'"

The fractures grew, as the press relayed of an Equal Rights Association meeting in 1868. "There were but two views on the question of suffrage; either it was a political arrangement to be given to and taken away from the people by the will of society or that it was a natural right," Elizabeth Stanton declared.

"In the evening a meeting was held in which a lively debate took place between Frederick Douglass, Reverend Olympia Brown, Susan B. Anthony and Lucy Stone, in relation to the advocacy of Negro and woman suffrages by the Republican Party."

Abolitionist leader Frederick Douglass thought that the "Republican Party was, far in advance of the Democrats, not only in relation to Negro suffrage but also woman suffrage." Anthony and Stanton disagreed, because the Republicans refused to add women's suffrage to their platform. A newspaper understated the growing tension. "The discussion did not end in any good results."

Anthony and Stanton realized they were playing a game of subtraction. They'd lost a key ally. Senator Sumner, who'd previously presented their petitions for abolition, sheepishly presented a petition to the Senate from one of his constituents for women's suffrage. He called it "untimely and injudicious."

On New Year's Day in 1868, Susan wrote a diary entry that spelled out the subtraction equation she faced. "All the old friends, with scarce an exception, are sure we are wrong. Only time can tell, but I believe we are right." Many of those who'd supported them before "engaged in bitterly denouncing the women for not repudiating their own cause."

The addition of a new member to their team created much division. Anthony and Stanton had accepted financial support from a controversial Democrat. "George Francis Train, a wealthy and eccentric Democrat, had volunteered as a helper . . . and had stirred up much irritation among Republicans by his witty and pungent comparisons of the relative qualifications for the vote of white women and black men." While trying to woo Southern Democrats at the time, the comparison was unfair for many reasons, especially because freed slaves had been denied an education while in slavery. Literary tests as voting requirements would become an unjust weapon against black suffrage in the decades to come.

Train became the financial backer of the new national women's suffrage newspaper called the *Revolution* that Anthony managed and Stanton edited. Its motto reflected a balanced equation: "Men, their rights, nothing more; women, their rights, nothing less."

Because of their relationship with Train, Anthony and Stanton were criticized. "Since the two men who had become its financial sponsors were Democrats, Mrs. Stanton and Miss Anthony were charged with deserting the slave and enlisting with 'copperheads and traitors.'"

How did they respond to the charge? "Because we make a higher demand than either Republicans or Abolitionists, they in self-defense revenged themselves by calling us Democrats . . . If claiming the right of suffrage for every citizen, male and female, black and white, a platform far above that occupied by Republicans or Abolitionists today, is to be a Democrat then we glory in the name, but we have not so understood the policy of modern Democracy."

Yet, there was a form of racism also working against them. If Anthony and Stanton's position had taken root in the Fourteenth or Fifteenth Amendment, women, regardless of color, would have earned the right to vote along with black men. The members of Congress who prioritized black suffrage were only prioritizing black men. They were discriminating against black women. So if the label of racist applies, even in a nuanced way, it applies to their opponents, too.

Stanton and Anthony's advocacy for abolishing slavery—including gathering over 300,000 names on petitions that gave Lincoln and the Thirteenth Amendment a mandate—needs to be taken into consideration when evaluating the totality of their contributions and views on race. Whatever Train's influence was on them, pain was their motivator to accept his financial help. They felt pain that Congress had let them down, pain that Senator Sumner and other friends had betrayed them, pain that their supporter Wendell Phillips had asked them to stand aside when he said, "One idea for a generation to come up in the order of their importance. First, Negro suffrage, then temperance, then the eight-hour movement, then woman suffrage. Three generations hence, woman suffrage will be in order." The women were insulted at being deemed less significant.

The Fifteenth Amendment was needed for a critical reason. Recently freed slaves were being targeted with violence, including lynching. Negro suffrage was needed to save lives. Yet the Fifteenth Amendment didn't protect freed female slaves when Congress passed it on February 26, 1869. It outlawed disfranchisement on account of race, color, or previous condition of servitude, but not sex.

The biggest obstacle facing Susan and the suffragists was politics, plain and simple. "Once Mrs. Stanton, lecturing in California, met Senator Bingham of Ohio stumping the state on behalf of the 14th and 15th Amendments which that state had declined to ratify. Mrs. Stanton gently charged him with insincerity, since every argument he was presenting applied equally to woman suffrage. With a cynical smile, he replied that he was not the puppet of logic but the slave of practical politics."

Politics had led to the use of delicate technical terms in order to ratify the Fifteenth Amendment. "Impartial suffrage had come into use to express the delicate discriminations intended, the inclusion in the electorate of Negroes and the exclusion of Northern white women and Southern white traitors." Universal suffrage meant suffrage for all regardless of sex or race.

"The moral courage of statesmen, but recently contending in exalted phrase for human liberty and equal rights for all, had utterly surrendered to the politician's eternal plea of expediency."

Substituting sex for race in the Fifteenth Amendment, Congressman George Julian of Indiana introduced a women's suffrage measure to become the Sixteenth Amendment on March 15, 1869. But the political will was gone. The flower waiting for the bee had closed. The public and political will was exhausted.

The American Equal Rights Association dissolved. Two organizations emerged: the National Woman Suffrage Association led by Stanton and Anthony and the American Woman Suffrage Association led by Lucy Stone. The equation of suffrage was now divided. What does a leader need in this situation? A new tactic, or in this former teacher's case, a new lesson plan.

Susan B. Anthony, age 28
(Wikimedia Commons)

Susan B. Anthony, age 28
(Library of Congress)

6
SWITCHING TACTICS

What must leaders do when external forces change everything? Whether facing a pandemic or a war or something less ominous such as a new technology, life often requires new tactics or a change in strategy. Such was the calculation Susan B. Anthony made in her effort to give women the right to vote.

"Susan B. Anthony in trouble"[6] was the headline in the *New York Herald* on November 16, 1872.

What crime had she committed? Trespassing? Robbery? Murder? No. She had voted. Eleven days earlier on November 5, Susan and more than a dozen women had voted in Rochester, New York, in the 1872 presidential election. Her choice for president was Ulysses S. Grant.

She was arrested by a U.S. marshal on the criminal charge of "having voted without having a lawful right to vote." What had changed? Her strategy. Because she was a U.S. citizen, she believed that she could vote based on the first section of the

---

[6] *New York Herald,* Nov. 16, 1872. See page 196 for this chapter's endnotes.

Fourteenth Amendment to the Constitution. She decided to try a new tactic. Maybe, just maybe, she could get the Supreme Court to see the justice of her position.

The newspapers soon weighed in on her case.

"There was nothing in the nature of an intended fraud in what the ladies did. They went to the polls without any disguise or deception; and if their votes were cast in contravention of the law, the person's really in default are the election officials," Philadelphia's *Public Ledger* opined on December 27, 1872. "Hence, to be trying to make an example of Miss Anthony and her female supporters is a farce."

Pomeroy's Democrat of New York went further on January 25, 1873. "Poor Susan B. Anthony is being courted by Uncle Sam. Susan wanted the right to ballot, so she voted. Then Uncle Sam went for her, and she was confined," an editorial complained about the 53-year-old Anthony. "This is an outrage on an old woman, and no good will come of it. Let the government look after the frauds committed by men, so-called, and let women have the right of suffrage. The country would be better off."

When the annual National Woman Suffrage convention met in January 1873, Anthony outlined several tactics for securing the vote: "by state constitutional amendments, to be adopted by electors at the polls, by a federal constitutional amendment to be adopted by a two-thirds vote of both Houses of the Congress and ratified by three-fourths of the state Legislatures, or, by taking their right under the Fourteenth Amendment."

She believed it was necessary to test this in court. "The vaults in yonder Capitol," said she, "hold the petitions of 100,000 women for a declaratory act; and the calendars of our courts show that many women are already testing their right to vote under the Fourteenth Amendment. I stand here under indictment for having exercised my right as a citizen to vote at the last election, and by a fiction of the law I am now in custody and not a free person."

Susan was crafty in her defense. Wanting to influence potential jurors, she embarked on a public-relations speaking tour. "Miss Anthony held a meeting in every post office district of her county (Monroe), 29 in number, speaking upon the subject, 'Is it a crime for a United States citizen to vote?'"

Displeased with her tactics, the U.S. district attorney moved her case to another county twenty-two days before her trial was to begin. Undeterred, she held twenty-one meetings in that county, and another suffragist held sixteen meetings.

The trial arrived on June 17, 1873. Filling the courtroom were notable politicians and attorneys, including former president Millard Fillmore. Several statements stood out, starting with that of Anthony's attorney, Judge Henry Selden.

"Miss Anthony believed and was advised that she had a right to vote under the provisions of the Federal Constitutional Amendments. She was advised as clearly that the question of her right could not be brought before the courts for trial without her voting or offering to vote. Her motives were pure and noble and carried no intent of fraud or crime," Selden argued. "If by the laws of her country she shall be condemned a criminal for taking the only step by which it was possible to bring the great constitutional question of her right before the courts for adjudication, it adds another reason to those I have advanced to show that women need the ballot for their protection."

She drew on the Fourteenth Amendment: "All persons born or naturalized in the United States, and subject to the jurisdiction thereof, are citizens of the United States and of the State wherein they reside. No State shall make or enforce any law which shall abridge the privileges or immunities of citizens of the United States; nor shall any State deprive any person of life, liberty, or property, without due process of law; nor deny to any person within its jurisdiction the equal protection of the laws."

What was more stunning, however, was how the presiding judge handled the jury and the verdict. Judge Ward Hunt directed the jury to render a guilty verdict. He didn't allow jurors to deliberate or contemplate the evidence. When Selden protested, Hunt refused to poll the jurors, who had some non-guilty votes. Instead he dismissed the jury.

Then Judge Hunt shocked the courtroom when he retrieved a written opinion from his pocket, one he had clearly prepared before he'd heard any of the arguments.

"Miss Anthony knew that she was a woman and that the constitution of this state prohibits her from voting," he stated. "The right of voting or the privilege of voting is a right or privilege arising under the Constitution of the state, and not that of the United States," Judge Hunt read from his prepared statement. "If the right belongs to any particular person, it is because such is entitled to it as a citizen of the state where he offers to exercise it, and not because of his citizenship of the United States." The fallout was fierce.

"There was widespread condemnation of Judge Hunt's conduct of the case, and none were more outspoken than some members of the jury who boldly declared that had they had the opportunity, they would not have voted guilty," a suffragist reflected in *Woman Suffrage and Politics*.

Even attorneys who did not support women's suffrage believed that the judge abused his power by taking the case from the jury and directing a guilty verdict. The next day, Judge Hunt ordered Susan B. Anthony to stand.

"Has the prisoner anything to say why sentence shall not be pronounced?" he asked.

"Yes, your Honor, I have many things to say; for in your ordered verdict of guilty, you have trampled underfoot every vital principle of our government. My natural rights, my civil rights, my political rights, my judicial rights, are all alike ignored," she began.

"Robbed of the fundamental privilege of citizenship, I am degraded from the status of a citizen to that of a subject; and not only myself individually, but all my sex are, by your Honor's verdict doomed to political subjection under this so-called republican form of government."

Hunt was not happy. "The court cannot listen to a rehearsal

of argument which the prisoner's counsel has already consumed three hours in presenting," he said.

Maintaining her respect and decorum, she kept talking in the spirit of one of the nation's founders.

"May it please your Honor, I am not arguing the question, but simply stating the reasons why sentence cannot in justice be pronounced against me. Your denial of my citizen's right to vote is the denial of my right of consent as one of the governed, the denial of my right of representation as one taxed, the denial of my right to a trial by jury of my peers as an offender against law; therefore, the denial of my sacred right to life, liberty, property, and—"

"The court cannot allow the prisoner to go on," Hunt said, interrupting her.

"But, your Honor will not deny me this one and only poor privilege of protest against this highhanded outrage upon my citizen's rights. May it please the Court to remember that since the day of my arrest last November, this is the first time that either myself or any person of my disfranchised class has been allowed a word of defense before judge or jury," she continued.

"The prisoner must sit down, the court cannot allow it," Hunt said, refusing to refer to her as a defendant.

She persisted. "Of all my persecutors from the corner grocery politician who entered the complaint, to the United States marshal, commissioner, district attorney, district judge, your Honor on the bench, not one is my peer, but each and all are my political sovereigns. . . . Precisely as no disfranchised person is entitled to sit upon the jury and no woman is entitled to the franchise, so none but a regularly admitted lawyer is allowed to practice in the courts, and no woman can gain admission to the bar—hence, jury, judge, counsel, all must be of superior class."

"The court must insist—the prisoner has been tried according to the established forms of law," the judge said.

"Yes, your Honor, but by forms of law, all made by men, interpreted by men, administered by men, in favor of men and against women; and hence your Honor's ordered verdict of guilty, against a United States citizen for the exercise of the 'citizen's right to vote,' simply because that citizen was a woman and not a man. . . . As then the slaves who got their freedom had to take it over or under or through the unjust forms of the law, precisely so now must women take it to get their right to a voice in this government; and I have taken mine, and mean to take it at every opportunity."

"The court orders the prisoner to sit down. It will not allow another word," Hunt insisted.

"When I was brought before your Honor for trial I hoped for a broad interpretation of the Constitution and its recent amendments, which should declare all United States citizens under its protecting aegis. . . . But failing to get this justice, failing even to get a trial by a jury—not of my peers—I ask not leniency at your hands but rather the full rigor of the law."

"The sentence of the Court is that you pay a fine of $100 and the costs of the prosecution," he declared.

"May it please your Honor, I will never pay a dollar of your unjust penalty. . . . And I shall earnestly and persistently continue to urge all women to the practical recognition of the old Revolutionary maxim, 'Resistance to tyranny is obedience to God.'"

"Madam, the court will not order you stand committed until the fine is paid," Hunt answered.

She did not pay her fine. But because he would not put her in prison—despite referring to her as the prisoner—she could not appeal her case to the U.S. Supreme Court, which is what she had wanted. Had the jury been allowed to deliberate or had the U.S. Supreme Court heard her case, especially because of the trial's irregularities and lack of due process, history might have been different. A year later, however, the U.S. Supreme court ruled in *Minor v. Happersett* that female citizens were not legally entitled to vote.

"She was a shrewd tactician; with prophetic insight, without compromise," a suffragist reflected on the secret behind Anthony's leadership skills. "Susan B. Anthony's aim was the national enfranchisement of women. As soon as she became convinced that the Constitution would have to be specifically amended to include woman suffrage, she set herself to this gigantic task. For a quarter of a century she appealed to Congress for action and to party conventions for suffrage endorsement."

In 1878, Senator Aaron A. Sargent, a Republican from California, introduced the Sixteenth Amendment to Congress, which would have extended the right to vote to women. This former teacher invoked a strategy of addition as she labored for this cause, especially in 1884.

The Women's Rights Convention met in March of that year in Washington, D.C. In addition to giving speeches, filing reports, and education members, they leveraged some new opportunities to make their case, as the newspapers relayed.

"The delegates to the women's convention, headed by Susan B. Anthony, were formally received by the president Thursday. Miss Anthony, who looks as bright, vigorous and untiring as ever, settled her gold-bow glasses firmly on her nose and began to talk as soon as they were marched up in front of the president's desk in his library," the *Kalamazoo Gazette* in Michigan reported on March 8, 1884, of the meeting between Susan B. Anthony and President Chester Arthur.

"The president stood up during the talk, his eyes twinkling humorously as the veteran agitators gathered about him. Miss Anthony's line of thought, clearly and vigorously expressed, was to the effect that if the president expected to be elected for another term of four years he would take a long step on the road by promising to put in his next message, if elected, a paragraph in favor of a 16th Amendment to the Constitution confirming the right of suffrage upon women."

How did President Arthur respond?

"The president was equal to the occasion. He said first in a very graceful way that he was glad to have the opportunity of meeting so many distinguish ladies, and then added that he was very confident they would secure all the rights they ought to have," the *Kalamazoo Gazette* article continued.

"This answer did not satisfy the blunt Miss Anthony. She said sharply: 'should not women have full equality in political rights with the men?'

"Miss Anthony, we would probably differ as to the details in answering that question," Arthur answered diplomatically, dodging a direct answer. Little did the women know, but Arthur had decided not to run for reelection. The death of his wife shortly before he was elected vice president had taken a toll on him. They could no longer hope to leverage presidential politics to win him over.

Another newspaper made fun of their efforts by reporting a humorous moment instead of taking the suffragists seriously.

"A polygamous discussion between Susan B. Anthony and Delegate Caine" was the headline in Washington's *Daily Critic* on March 10, 1884. This was followed by: "Susan B. Anthony and Delegate Caine of Utah had quite a lively tilt on the subject of polygamy."

How did she respond to the issue of men having multiple wives, which was a religious practice in Utah at the time? "Miss Anthony took the ground that it was the men who wanted six and seven wives; that no woman ever wanted six or seven men," the article said.

"Mr. Caine argued that the plurality of wives was simply the result of religious conviction, and that women enter into it the same as they entered a convent."

Another satirical article came from a representative from the West.

"Susan B. Anthony has been in Washington some time canvassing among congressman in behalf of female suffrage. One day last week she encountered a new member from the far West who, being introduced to her, broke out in the following fashion: 'Glad to make your acquaintance, Mrs. Anthony. Saw your son in the Senate the other day. Looks a little broken down. Nevermind that. Ought to feel proud of him. Guess he'll last as long as Rhode Island,'" *The Sun* of Gunnison, Colorado, reported on March 15, 1884. The congressman referred to in the article was Senator Henry B. Anthony of Rhode Island.

"And without giving the venable virgin time to recover from her astonishment the bumptious representative of the sage-grass regions disappeared in the crowd," the article said.

Despite this ridicule, another newspaper told the real story. Suffragists were testifying at a House committee hearing, a big step.

"Miss Susan B. Anthony and a delegation of women suffragists waited up on the House Judiciary Committee this morning to make an appeal in behalf of universal suffrage. Miss Anthony, Mrs. Caroline Miller, Miss Clay (the daughter of CM Clay the Kentucky Statesman) and a number of others addressed the committee. The committee listened with attention to all the arguments," Washington's *Evening Star* reported on March 8, 1884.

"After concluding their argument before the committee some of the women suffragists laid hold of individual members of Congress whenever they could find them, and labored to impress them of the justice of their cause."

In 1887, the U.S. Senate defeated the Sixteenth Amendment, otherwise known as the Anthony amendment. Not giving up, the women added another strategy and tactic by focusing on winning over one state at a time.

"When, however, she saw that Congress was obdurate, as an able and intensely practical leader she temporarily directed the main energy of the suffrage movement to trying to win individual states," a suffragist later reflected about Susan's strategy.

Time healed some wounds. In 1890, the two national suffrage organizations merged, forming the National American Women's Suffrage Association. Anthony became its president in 1902, after Elizabeth Cady Stanton.

They lived to see some success. As a territory, Wyoming gave women the right to vote in 1869 and retained it after a bitter debate in Congress when Wyoming became a state in 1890. Three other states followed: Colorado in 1893, Utah 1896, and Idaho 1896. The suffragists had witnessed cultural improvements. Unlike at the World Anti-Slavery Conference in 1840 that Stanton had attended, it was now acceptable for women to speak in public, as Anthony and others had proven multiple times. More and more women were attending college. More employment options were available to women.

Elizabeth Cady Stanton died October 26, 1902. Four days before her death, she dictated a letter to President Theodore Roosevelt, and the day before her death, she dictated a letter to Roosevelt's wife, Edith. While grieving, Susan stepped in and wrote a letter to Roosevelt on November 28.

"Dear Mr. President: It was most beautiful and appropriate that the last act of Mrs. Elizabeth Cady Stanton should have been to appeal to the President of the United States for a recognition of that right which she had la bored over half-a-century to obtain for women. It had been in my mind for some time to repeat a similar plea which I made to you a year ago, and since the death of my loved co-worker I have thought daily that I would add my sanction to her last words," she wrote. On her mind was his annual message to Congress, which is known today as the State of the Union address.

"I realize that at this hour your message is finished, and I await with extreme anxiety to learn if Mrs. Stanton's request has had the effect of securing even the smallest recognition of woman in that important document. . . . A word from you, President Roosevelt, on any phase of the woman suffrage question would be of inestimable benefit and would give it a prestige and a sanction which would carry it immeasurably forward," the 82-year-old Anthony wrote, asking him to mention women's suffrage in his annual address to Congress. By this time, she had retired as president of the National American Women's Suffrage Association.

"It would be as noble an act as the Emancipation Proclamation of Abraham Lincoln, and would render you immortal. I need not suggest to you the immense advantage it would be if women could carry their cause to the legislatures instead of to the electorate. I assure you that, with the incentive of this recommendation, the women of the country would roll up a petition which would give you and the Congress the support of a million names," she wrote, noting that he was the only president who'd ever offered them even the slightest hope.

Roosevelt didn't mention suffrage in his annual message to Congress. He did, however, come to support women's suffrage after his time as president, during his failed third-party run for the presidency in 1912.

Susan knew they had to find a way to turn women's suffrage into a political expediency, a political advantage for politicians. This former teacher recognized that their biggest foe was an equation of power and politics.

"So long as you and I and all women are political slaves, it ill becomes us to meddle with the weightier discussions of our sovereign masters. It will be quite time enough for us, with self-respect, to declare ourselves for or against any party upon the intrinsic merit of its policy, when men shall recognize us as their political equals," Susan wrote to Lucy Stone, her former rival.

"If all the suffragists of all the states could see eye to eye on this point, and stand shoulder to shoulder against every party and politician not fully and unequivocally committed to 'Equal Rights for Women,' we should become at once the moral balance of power which could not fail to compel the party of highest intelligence to proclaim woman suffrage the chief plank of its platform," she wrote. "Until that good day comes, I shall continue to invoke the party in power, and each party struggling to get into power, to pledge itself to the emancipation of our enslaved half of the people."

Susan B. Anthony died on March 13, 1906. A new generation of suffragists would emerge. They would reveal important life secrets, including perseverance on a spring.

Elizabeth Cady Stanton & Susan B.
Anthony, circa 1880 (Library of Congress)

7
PERSEVERANCE ON A SPRING

What is resilience? In shorthand, it's the ability to snap back quickly after a setback. Resilience is perseverance on a spring or courage on a coil. Life requires long-term perseverance and short-term resilience. Two suffragists stand out for sharing this important skill.

Though more than twenty years separated them in age, these two suffragists had much in common. Both challenged cultural expectations by achieving an education. Both practiced journalism to make their mark. Both tapped the power of advertising, the newest form of social media and mass communication, to carve a brand and present their case for reform. Both leveraged tabloids to their advantage. Despite these remarkable similarities, they couldn't have begun life more differently. One was born a socialite, the other a slave. Both were called martyrs. Who were they?

"While women have figured among the thousands of martyrs, who have sacrificed home, even life, to a noble cause . . . but one has risen. . . . She is Ida B. Wells,"[7] the *Boston Herald* declared in 1892.

Born into slavery in Holly Springs, Mississippi, on July 16, 1862, by age fourteen she was a teacher in a country school.

---

[7] *Boston Herald quoted in Columbia Herald (TN)*, Dec. 23, 1892. See page 197 for this chapter's endnotes.

How was this possible? After the Civil War, the Freedman's Aid Society opened a school in Asbury Methodist Episcopal Church in Holly Springs for children and adults of all ages. Attending the school that later became Rust College, Ida emerged a teacher, and she later became a journalist. Moving to Memphis at age twenty-two, she taught school and attended Fisk University in Nashville. Within a decade, she'd become an activist known throughout the nation for surviving a mob attack on her office and her free speech rights.

What had elevated her to near-martyrdom? As the *Boston Herald* described, Ida had "for the public good (so she conscientiously thought) assassinated the Marats of Memphis in a fiery denunciation editorial, condemning the barbaric lawlessness of lynching in *The Free Speech*, of which she was the editor."

After losing her teaching job because of an article she wrote criticizing the limited education options for freed Africans, she bounced back and became a full-time journalist. When three of her friends were lynched in March 1892, she investigated the case, wrote an article, and published her findings, exposing the injustice and horror of lynching. She lost her job and home as a result. The *Free Speech* office was destroyed. With her life under threat, she fled Memphis.

"Like all martyrs to a cause, the torrent of her convictions swept away all cautiousness and today she is an exile from her home and threatened with hanging or burning at the stake, should she return in twenty years by the lawless mob she denounced in the *Free Speech*," the *Boston Herald* wrote, concluding that "the salvation of the colored people of the South may come through a woman."

An anonymous writer in a Tennessee newspaper condemned her, calling her a wench and harlot, and denounced her martyrdom. How did she bounce back from being driven from her home in Tennessee? How was she resilient? She tapped the power of the tabloid—and it's not what you might think.

A tabloid appeared in the *Washington Bee* newspaper on October 29, 1892. Featuring a photograph of Ida B. Wells, it highlighted in bold print, "Speaking at Metropolitan A.M.E. church, 'Southern Mob Rule' the Simple Story of an Eloquent Woman."

Similar to a sponsored news story today, this was an advertisement disguised as a news article. It was a tabloid, which meant it was condensed. Unlike today, when tabloids refer to a certain type of sensational newspaper lacking credibility, tabloids in the 1890s were credible advertisements, usually with pictures and often with paragraphs of text. This one about Ida used testimonials from her previous speeches.

"All eyes were turned on Ida B. Wells, for it was she, herself a victim of the portrayed outrages and she was moved to grief. Miss Wells was the star of the convention. Though modest in appearance she shone with intellectual brilliancy," the *Washington Bee* ad began.

"Miss Wells made a national reputation as editor of the Memphis *Free Speech*, the publication of which she was compelled to suspend because of her bold fearless and intelligent denunciation of mob violence and the enactment and enforcement of malicious and degrading civil law."

Instead of hiding from the mob that had killed her friends, she had embarked on a speaking tour of the Northeast. She frequently spoke at churches of the A.M.E., the denomination that had established the school in her hometown where she had received an education.

"As a platform orator, Miss Wells takes high and commanding rank as an earnest and eloquent speaker. No woman of the race has greater power than she possesses to hold the attention of an audience," the tabloid in the *Washington Bee* continued. "In a public address before the African American League at Knoxville in July 1891, she astonished her hearers by her impassioned denunciation of the separate bar law and mob rule.

"In her lecture on the African-American in literature delivered before the Concord literary Circle of Brooklyn New York, September 15, 1892, she completely captivated the large and cultivated audience."

The praise continued, "At the testimonial tendered her by the women of New York City and Brooklyn at Lyric Hall New York October 5, 1892, she moved the vast assemblage to tears by the pathetic recital of the terrible lynching of three of her friends at Memphis, in March 1892, and the forced suspension of her newspaper." This ad-article was submitted by the minister of the church in Washington where she was to speak.

Her speaking did not stop in the fall of 1892. She went on a speaking tour in England, published a book based on her investigative reporting on lynching, moved to Chicago, married journalist Ferdinand Barnett, and had four children.

None of this would have been possible without resiliency. By springing back from adversity, she made a difference.

"Miss Ida B. Wells, the greatest race defender of her time and among the noblest of women," the *Afro-American Advocate* praised her on June 30, 1893.

She continued her journalism and activism, including becoming a champion of a new organization, the National Association for the Advancement of Colored People. Though she wrote numerous articles, one in particular stands out for its perspective on voting and explains why she became an advocate for women's suffrage. For her, women's suffrage was a matter of life and death.

Why did Ida Wells want women to get the right to vote? Why did she want the Fifteenth Amendment to be enforced? To her, it was a matter of preserving her race. "How enfranchisement stops lynching" was the title of her article published in *Original Rights* magazine in June 1910. Unlike the dense, column-to-column newspapers of the 1700s and 1800s, in which almost every word on the page was the same height, the newspapers and magazines of the early 1900s reflected the need for speed. Headlines and subheads were larger than the main text allowing users to scan for articles that interested them. Magazines were all the rage during this era, populated with articles and advertisements, reproduced photographs and drawn tableaux pictures that told a story in one image.

Published monthly by Charles Lenz of New York, *Original Rights* magazine sold for twenty-five cents. After guessing the origins of slavery in the United States, Ida viewed the Civil War as the turning point that fulfilled the ideals of the American Revolution.

"The flower of the 19th century civilization for the American people was the abolition of slavery and the enfranchisement of all manhood. Here at last was squaring of practice with precept, with true democracy, with the Declaration of Independence and with the Golden Rule."

She believed the disgrace of the twentieth century was making the Thirteenth and Fourteenth amendments a mockery or "an absolute dead letter in the Constitution." Referring to the South, she declared that a third of the states had made laws that abridged the life, liberty, and pursuit of happiness of "persons of Negro descent."

"The right of citizens is denied and abridged in these states on account of race, color, and previous condition of servitude and has been so denied ever since the withdrawal of United States troops from the South. This in spite of the 15th Amendment which declares no state shall do this."

While the Thirteenth Amendment had freed slaves in the South and the Fourteenth Amendment had given them citizenship, the Fifteenth Amendment had given freed black men but not women the right to vote. This proved more theoretical than actually practiced. The reason? The Ku Klux Klan.

"These rights were denied first by violence and blood shed, the Ku Klux Klan who during the first years after the Civil War murdered Negroes wholesale, for attempting to exercise the rights given by these amendments and for trusting the government, which was powerful enough to give them the ballot, to be strong enough to protect them in its exercise."

Referring to a speech by Senator Benjamin Tillman of South Carolina, she told about him shooting freed slaves to keep them from voting and throwing out the ballot boxes of African Americans. She talked about how the federal government had abandoned them by allowing discriminatory Jim Crow laws to stand.

Then she gave a passionate plea for voting. "With no sacredness of the ballot there can be no sacredness of life itself. For if the strong can take the weak man's ballot, when it suits his purpose to do so, he will take his life also." She called trial by jury a mockery. "The mob says: 'the people have no vote with which to punish us or the consenting officers of the law, therefore we indulge our brutal instincts, give free reign to race prejudice and lynch, hang, and burn them as we please.'"

She tied suppressing black votes to increased physical violence and lynching. "Therefore the more complete the disenfranchisement more frequent and has been the hangings, shootings and burnings."

Introducing data, she explained that in 1882, fifty-two people were lynched. Within ten years, after Jim Crow laws had suppressed the votes of free African males, 252 people were lynched. After she went public with this information, lynching began to decline steadily over the next decade until 1902, when they started to increase again, even in Illinois, Lincoln's home state, which was more tolerant than some.

Then African-American male voters succeeded in getting an anti-lynching law passed Illinois in 1905. The new law required a sheriff to lose his job if he allowed a mob to lynch a suspect. Much of Ida's lynching research had focused on the suppression of witnesses favorable to suspects. She showed her political savvy by using data collected from white journalists to make her case.

After the 1905 anti-lynching law, a black and a white man

were lynched in Cairo, Illinois. As the law required, the sheriff lost his job for failing to prevent the lynching. Going to Cairo, Ida investigated and interviewed witnesses. The sheriff did not get his job back and the law was followed, setting an example of the cost to sheriffs who gave in to mob rule.

The next time a mob attempted to lynch a man in another Illinois town, the sheriff remembered the outcome of the Cairo case. He refused to let the mob take the suspect. The result was accountability. The voters of Illinois, including African-American men, held their lawmakers accountable and stopped barbaric lynching.

"It is believed that with this decision 'mob law can have no place in Illinois' has given lynching a death blow in this state." This success gave her hope that women could hold their government accountable if given the right to vote.

Little did Ida B. Wells-Barnett know when she wrote this article in 1910 that within three years her resiliency would be tested in front of more than 300,000 people in Washington, D.C.

★ ★ ★ ★ ★

"Harvard bars suffragette" was the headline in October 1909 in the *Elkhart Daily Review* in Indiana, as well as in papers across the United States. "Miss Milholland, Vassar graduate, refused admittance to law school. . . She was denied admittance solely on the ground that she is a woman and the belief by Harvard officials that men and women should not study together."

Born in 1886, twenty-three-year-old Inez Milholland's name was familiar to New York's high-society crowd. But this time she was at the center of a national news story when Harvard Law School rejected her as a law student.

This wasn't the first time that school authorities had denied her something she wanted. One setback took place at Vassar College when she was a student. How did she respond when Vassar wouldn't let her use the chapel for a suffrage event? She snapped back like a spring, undeterred.

"One of her acts during this period was to hold a suffrage meeting in a graveyard at night when permission to hold the meeting in the college chapel had been refused her," her obituary recalled.

Those who knew of Inez's resilience weren't surprised at what she did after Harvard rejected her law-school application. She soon thereafter made headlines again.

"Inez Milholland Arrested" was the all-cap headline in the *New York Sun* on December 4, 1909, followed by this subhead: She was protecting shirtwaist striker's pickets.

A shirtwaist was a ready-to-wear button-down blouse popular in the early part of the twentieth century. Manhattan was home to 450 textile factories employing more than 400,000 workers, which included hundreds of shirtwaist workers who worked twelve-hour days in cramped conditions. Many were immigrants. She joined the picket line of female employees in the shirtwaist strike. These female factory workers were seeking higher wages.

"Since the shirtwaist makers have been on strike, Miss Milholland has been much interested in their cause and frequently establishes herself as a volunteer picket outside factories to make sure that the police do not make arrests that are not justified."

Did she ever make it to law school? Her father's alma mater, New York University, admitted her to law school.

Were all of these headlines the result of serendipity? No. Many stemmed from Inez's ability to feed the hungry press juicy tidbits. She first learned about the news business from her father, who edited the *New York Tribune* for a dozen years and became active in Republican politics. He became wealthy after investing in the new technology of vacuum tubes, which today are used by banks to transport bank tubes at drive-through tellers. Back then, the technology was used by the postal system in New York. The investment made the Mulholland family very wealthy.

The result was that Inez had the means and know-how to

garner much publicity, whether by opening a law office or flying in an airplane. She knew how to get attention in the media.

Like Ida Wells-Barnett, Inez leveraged the tabloid to bring fresh attention to women's suffrage and her new tactic. By putting out a tabloid in advance of the big event it advertised, she became the face—the cover girl—of the new women's suffrage movement that would soon battle President Woodrow Wilson.

The fifth page of the *Salt Lake Telegram* on March 3, 1913, was mostly columns of text. In the middle was a portrait of Inez Milholland, seated, wearing a nice dress and holding a scroll. At first glance, Inez's picture and the accompanying text looked like an advertisement. Further inspection revealed that the copy was written by Inez for an important occasion. The women's suffrage movement was getting a reboot.

"Every principal, however splendid, needs advocating, declares Miss Milholland," the headline proclaimed, followed by this subhead: "That is what the suffrage parade in Washington today is expected to do for woman suffrage"

"Washington, March 3. Several thousand women, representing all classes of women from the little factory worker to the woman of leisure, and from every state in the union, march this afternoon in the national capital to bring home to the minds of the National lawmakers the strength and earnestness of the suffrage movement in this country," Inez wrote.

Then her article took a surprising turn. Rather than immediately discussing the merits of giving women the right to vote, she explained their new methodology.

"This is an age of advertising. Every principal today, no matter how splendid, requires advertising presented to the minds of the commonwealth. Every politician advertises his principles by various ways and means."

Then she discussed what was happening in Washington. As

readers across the nation read her pre-planned article on March 3, 1913, Inez and 8,000 women from across the United States were marching in a women's suffrage parade in Washington D.C. The parade was an advertisement for members of Congress and the incoming president, Woodrow Wilson.

"This is what the wonderful suffrage pageant today is expected to do for the principal involved. It will present to the minds of men who are too busy to peruse our literature and attend our meetings the deep significance of the movement," she wrote. "It will present to their imagination in tabloid form the idea we wish to convey that women of all classes are standing shoulder to shoulder for a high principal."

Just as a picture of Ida with testimonials was designed to bring people to hear her speak at the Metropolitan A.M.E. church in 1892, so Inez was applying the same technique to suffrage. Tabloids were succinct, giving readers the ability to understand at a glance.

"Realizing the value of advertising, we have taken unusual methods of imparting the information we wish to present to men who do not understand that we women want to represent ourselves in government. That women are deeply interested in the upbuilding and safeguarding of life, as men are interested in the building and safeguarding of property, and properly so."

She then made the suffrage movement personal to the reader.

"When men see their mothers, their friends, their women associates in business and the drawing room taking part in this big procession they cannot fail to realize that there must be some splendid purpose behind it. It will set them to thinking."

She took aim at a common sentiment and stereotype. Politics had become corrupted. Women's participation through voting would change that corruption, especially in the political machines of New York. This was personal to her, because her father had been forced out of politics when he took on the machine.

"The awakened interest in suffrage today is partly due to the fact that men have found out that through the municipal misconduct that has been brought to the light through the exposure of police system corruption of New York and the covering of the Barns machine in Albany and other shocking relations of misgovernment, something is wrong with our present system," she continued.

She aimed at the reader's intellect. "The thinking American today believes in equal suffrage. The average American man who thinks earnestly desires good government," she wrote, before using a stereotype to her advantage.

"As men know that women are not politically corruptible, it is natural for them to turn to the class of people who are noted for their absence of corrupt propensities. Men interested in good government are willing to turn to any group of people who promise a fundamental remedy."

She concluded by stating a positive outcome of women universally gaining the right to vote. "And men are beginning to realize that women represent an influence much to be desired in government."

Just as Inez paved the way for the parade in print, so did she pave the way for the parade in reality. Little did she realize when she wrote these words that she would demonstrate resilience on the spot at the front of the parade, and Ida would steal the show with the spring in her step. Ida and Inez would put the two *i*'s in resilience.

Ida B. Wells, 1893 by Mary Garrity (Wikimedia Commons).

IDA B. WELLS.

Ida B. Wells, 1891 newspaper image (Library of Congress)

Inez Milholland (Library of Congress)

Inez Milholland (Library of Congress)

8
RESILIENCE ON PARADE

"Miss Inez Milholland, the beautiful New York suffragette, who rode ahead of the great suffrage parade in Washington,"[8] the *Colorado Springs Gazette* reported about Inez's role in leading the grand women's suffrage parade on March 3, 1913, in Washington, D.C. Leveraging the timing of President Woodrow Wilson's inauguration the following day, on March 4, the National American Women's Suffrage Association hoped the parade would make national headlines, catch the attention of the people in town for the inauguration, and, most importantly, convince members of Congress to pass an amendment for women's voting rights.

Riding on a white horse, Inez was the second person in the parade behind the grand marshal. She stood out for her resemblance to an English herald from the era of chivalry. "Miss Milholland was costumed as a herald of ancient times, and carried a long trumpet, which she blew at intervals announcing the coming of woman's freedom," the press reported.

Like a masthead on a ship, she caught the attention of the

---

[8] *Colorado Springs Gazette,* March 4, 1913. See page 198 for this chapter's endnotes.

crowd and newspaper reporters. At least one gentleman had traveled from Pennsylvania just to see Inez. "A tall man groomed rustled up to an officer and inquired for Miss Milholland. When the officer pointed her out the man informed him that he had 'come all the way from Philadelphia to see her.' The last scene of him he was tramping silently but honestly behind her white horse."

Her costume in particular was notable. "Miss Inez Milholland, wearing a heavy white lace robe, over which was thrown a blue cloth cape, bearing a big yellow cross on her right, like a knight of old, led the parade mounted on a big white charger," the *Denver Post* reported with great detail. Inez, who was known for her athleticism at Vassar, wore a Wonder Woman–like crown, an image of women in the present and in the future.

"Her hair falling loosely over her shoulders was topped by a gold crown, over which hung a large gold star. Miss Milholland, represented the woman of the future, and as such gave a practical demonstration of what this sort of woman can accomplish."

Waiting for Inez at the Treasury Building was Hedwiga Reicher, a German silent film actress who portrayed Columbia. Reicher, "attired as 'Columbia' in the national colors and a liberty cap, stepped slowly from the shadows of the giant marble pillars on the porch of the Treasury."

Columbia heard the sounds of the parade "the crusade of women—and summoned to her side Justice, Charity, Liberty, Peace, and Hope all represented by prominent suffragettes attired in artistic flowing drapery."

Under the tune of the "Star-Spangled Banner" and while large U.S. flags unfurled on the roof, Columbia stood resilient with her staff topped by an eagle. Her Grecian robes bore the red stripes of the flag. Then with Inez leading on her horse, the parade unfolded like a documentary.

National American Women's Suffrage Association officers marched in front of the amendment float that declared: "We demand an amendment to the Constitution of the United States enfranchising the women of this country."

The parade showed American women as college graduates, wage earners, labor workers, business workers, government workers, and professionals, such as physicians, having them parade together in groups.

Many of these women carried memorable banners, such as: "Man and woman make the state but man alone rules the state." To counter the argument that women's suffrage would break up families, another banner declared: "We prepare our children for the state. Let us help the state prepare for our children." A large portion of the parade featured delegations of women representing their states.

Before the parade had advanced very far from the U.S. Capitol, Inez realized that she had big challenges in front of her. The police had failed to clear parts of Pennsylvania Avenue, the street on which they were marching, before the parade began. She saw mobs packing the street, especially near the U.S. Treasury Department, where the reviewing stand was set up. In addition, many unruly parade watchers hurled insults and assaulted some of the 8,000 women behind Inez. One threat seemed ripped from a newspaper comic strip.

"Word had gone out that 600 students from Georgetown University Collegiate Department were waiting up the line each with a pasteboard box under his arm and each box containing 10 live mice, which was to be liberated among the women marchers and bust up the proceedings," the *Washington Herald* reported.

"When the mice story reached Capitol Hill, at least two policemen in the reporters' range of vision got hold of trouser clips, such as the bicyclists' wear and made the lower end of their trousers mouse proof," the reporter observed of the metal clips used to protect pants from getting caught in a bicycle wheel.

"If anyone lets any mice loose here all I say that in this crush, Lord help them mice," a policeman in an automobile called out.

Worse than mice, whether real or rumored, was the packed crowd on the parade route.

The failure of the local police to clear the streets created a crisis, resulting in a delay and sending one hundred people to the hospital, according to initial newspaper reports. The parade organizers asked the federal government for help. The war secretary called in two troops of the U.S. cavalry from nearby Fort Myers.

Inez, however, stood out for her resilience and how she faced the packed streets obstructing the parade and the people hurling insults. Showing perseverance on a spring, she immediately took action and joined the police.

"Growing impatient at the long stops while the police try to clear a path for the marchers, Miss Milholland followed the example of the mounted police and charged into the crowds, calling upon them to desist from rowdyism and fall back."

She rebuked the rowdy ruffians. "At a cross street where the congestion represented a solid wall of humanity, Miss Milholland, riding into the crowd, which retreated a few paces and over the shaking head of her mount, addressed the men."

She chided them, "You men should be ashamed of yourselves standing there idly and permitting this sort of thing to continue. If you have a particle of backbone, you will come out here and help us to continue our parade instead of standing there and shouting at us."

The mob "fell back respectfully, apparently overcome at this dramatic and unexpected scolding. Then it burst into loud cheering for the courageous young woman." The *Washington Herald* put it this way: "Miss Inez Milholland, on a white steed at head of notable procession, cheered by thousands."

Some papers provided more detail. "Inez Milholland on white horse charges street mob," the *Cleburne Morning Review* of Cleburne, Texas, reported. She "rode up beside a mounted policeman, and helped to charge the crowd. Miss Milholland gesticulated and shouted at the mob and rode her horse into them with good effect."

Inez knew that behind her in the parade were dozens of advertisements in the form of parade vignettes that sought to tell the story of women's quest for voting. One included a banner depicting the beginning of the movement at the first women's rights conference in 1848. Despite the storytelling in the parade's costumes, banners, and floats, the headlines the next day were less about the plight of suffrage than the fright of the crowd.

"Women in big pageant, unprotected, battle through avenue, mobs" the *Washington Herald* declared, noting it was "a national disgrace." A subhead in the *Denver Post* focused on the mob: "Suffragists Insulted by Rowdies in Crowd." The newspaper published one of the best articles about "a mob of hooting, jeering men and boys, which the handful of police was unable to restrain." One press report estimated the crowd at 300,000.

Many in the mob were drunk. They hurled insults as the women paraded banners declaring sentiments such as, "Women have free fathers. Let men have free mothers." Banner holders were torn from women's hands and broken. The *Denver Post* reported an "instance of a hoodlum climbing on a float and insulting beautiful girl." Likewise, "a ruffian broke into the ranks and before she [granddaughter of Elizabeth Cady Stanton] could ward him off, grabbed her."

Some attacked the parade's section of women college graduates, who were dressed in caps and gowns. "The girls carrying the Vassar banner were rudely treated in their banner badly damaged."

Like Inez, some parade marchers fought back at times. "Angry women, resisting the insulting remarks made by the bystanders, struck at them with the flag sticks, and one woman, who refused to give her name, struck a man down."

Not even the wife and daughter of the outgoing president, President William Howard Taft, were respected by the ruffians in the crowd. "A group of hoodlums gathered directly in front of the reviewing stand, in which were Mrs. Taft and Miss Helen Taft and several other invited guests from the White House, and completely spoiled all the pleasure of the event by their insulting remarks. When it became evident that no attempt was to be made to remove the disorderly crowd, Mrs. Taft and the other members of the White House party left the stand."

The *Washington Herald* also reported an incident of internal conflict within the parade. The moment showed that not only did Inez have a resilient spring in her step, but so did Ida.

The reporter used a subhead to note that she "defies sentiment" during the parade. "Mrs. Ida Wells-Barnett . . ., who is one of the leaders of her race and has lectured in the cause of . . . in Europe and America, had come from Chicago in the Illinois delegation of women."

The largest portion of the parade was the delegation organized by states. A banner explained that some states had given women the right to vote: "Nine states of light among 39 in darkness." Among those were Wyoming, Colorado, Utah, Idaho, Washington, California, Arizona, Kansas, and Oregon.

After this followed women grouped in state delegations to emphasize the need for all American female citizens to vote. The point was to show that women from these non-suffrage states wanted the right to vote, just like the women from the West.

Ida's home state of Illinois was unusual compared with both the suffrage and non-suffrage states. Allowed to vote for school officials, women in Illinois had partial or incremental suffrage. They were not allowed to vote for president, their state legislators, or members of Congress. Women who voted for school officers were given a separate ballot and told to cast it in a separate ballot box.

Because Ida was a former slave, her position as a member of the Illinois delegation stood out. "But some of the marchers from the states farther south, had objected to her presence when the North and the South were lining up side-by-side, to await their places in the line."

How did Ida respond to their objections? On the surface, she seemed to swallow it. "Wherefore Mrs. Barnett quietly stepped aside and now stood back among onlookers."

Other women in the Illinois delegation, Virginia Brooks and Belle Squire supported Ida marching with them instead of joining the separate group of colored women marching in the back of the parade. A newsman approached Ida.

"But the Illinois women want me to march in their section," she smiled to the reporter, "and I shall. Illinois is Lincoln's state, you know. I don't believe Lincoln's state is going to permit Alabama or Georgia or any other state to dictate to it now. As Illinois comes along, I'll join them."

And she did. She waited with the crowd on the sidewalk near the start of the parade. When the Illinois delegation approached, she joined them and finished the parade with the Illinois ladies. Near the end, the parade also included a sorority from Howard University, an African-American college.

Several newspapers told her story. The *Cleveland Gazette* ran a picture of her with the news. "Mrs. Barnett not only braved the scorn of her Southern sisters (white) but enjoyed a period of publicity not to her liking but incident to the race feeling evident throughout the inaugural ceremony, Mrs. Barnett marched with the Illinois delegation and the colored prejudice in the inaugural parade was forever barred."

Chicago's *Broad Ax*, also reported the incident. "It might be also mentioned here that Mrs. Ida B. Wells-Barnett proudly marched with the head officials or with the head ladies of the Illinois delegation showing that no color line existed in any part of the first national parade of the noble women who are in favor of equal suffrage."

A few days later, the *Broad Ax* announced a fundraiser to pay for her travel expenses. Having sent her to Washington, the Alpha Suffrage Club hosted a night of entertainment honoring Ida and the two Illinois women who had stood beside her. Ida was pleased "to represent the race in the suffrage parade."

She had organized the Alpha Suffrage Club to give colored women an opportunity to study political and civic issues and "to get hold of every colored woman in the city of Chicago" for the cause of suffrage, as she put it.

Her decision to quickly bounce back from prejudice may seem anticlimactic compared to her more dramatic life-threatening brush with lynch mobs twenty years earlier. But she took a great risk during the national women's suffrage parade in D.C., especially considering that many in the mob watching the parade hurled insults and attacked some women.

The negative headlines about the mob at the parade and the stories of Ida and Inez gave the suffrage movement publicity, even if some of it was negative. At least one reporter concluded that the parade had met its goal.

"It was a day of tremendous significance as the suffragists achieved, beyond the realm of doubt, their purpose in putting the cause of woman suffrage so closely before the federal government that the government's chief men must try it for its merits," the *Washington Herald* journalist observed.

A few months later, in June 1913, the governor of Illinois gave Ida something that Inez of New York did not yet have: the right to vote for president. Illinois gave women the right to vote for president in 1913 but still prevented them from voting for their legislators. It was progress by the inches, though it made Illinois the first state east of the Mississippi River to give women the right to vote in a presidential election.

Inez's role as a herald of sorts continued. So did her resiliency. Appearing in other parades, including suffrage parades in New York, she married Eugene Boissevain in July 1913. When World War I broke out in Europe, she took her pacifist passions to the war front as a newspaper correspondent. She broke news the moment she stepped on England's soil. "A German submarine chased the American liner the *St. Paul,*" she reported. When she arrived in Liverpool, she sent a cable back to Philadelphia, which led the newspaper next door in Trenton, New Jersey, to connect her with the story. "Most beautiful suffragette says American liner *St. Paul* chased by German submarine," the *Trenton Evening Times* reported on June 2, 1915. The news was highly relevant. Less than a month earlier on May 7, a German U-boat had sunk a passenger liner, the *Lusitania*, eleven miles off Ireland's coast. Within twenty minutes, the ship and its 1,198 passengers and crew perished, including more than 128 Americans. The German embassy warned Americans against traveling to Europe, something Inez clearly wasn't heeding.

On board the ship incognito was Guglielmo Marconi, the famed Italian who discovered the science behind the wireless telegram, which is known today as the radio. The Germans were after him.

"I have this from the captain of the *Saint Paul*, who told it to Guglielmo Marconi and me just before we got off the boat in Liverpool on Saturday. I do not think it was known to any of the other passengers. It was known that there was likely to be an attempt made by submarine to stop the ship and take Marconi off."

They had removed Marconi's name from his luggage and lied about his name on the passenger list. "As we approached the war zone, rather elaborate precautions were taken to safeguard Marconi. There was a general tacit agreement among the passengers that if we were stopped by a submarine, we were all to 'lie like gentlemen.'"

Within a couple of months, her purpose in Europe had become clear. She was to be a herald of news about the war. "Mrs. Eugene Boissevain, the former Miss Inez Mulholland, noted suffragette and woman lawyer of New York, has been accorded the privilege of visiting the Italian fighting front with the first party of newspaper correspondents allowed to enter the zone where operations have been carried on," *Tulsa World* reported on August 31, 1915. "The Italian authorities have permitted no newspaper writers to visit the fighting front heretofore."

Tapping her activist instincts, Inez, however, wrote and

spoke too much about pacifism in this role. The Italian authorities sent her back to America. Bouncing back once again, she took on the role of herald for the suffrage movement.

Agreeing to travel through the western states in the autumn of 1916, Inez once again became a herald for suffrage. This time she would not be able to bounce back. Her lack of resilience was not due to a lack of courage but to a matter of medicine.

"The unenfranchised women of the nation appeal to you for help in their fight for political freedom. We appeal to you to help us, for you alone have both the power and will," Inez began in her 1916 stump speech. Though not running for office, she frequently repeated this speech while touring western states in October 1916.

By this time, the leaders of the Congressional Union, which had been the federal lobbying arm in Washington, D.C., for the National American Women's Suffrage Association (NAWSA), had left to create a new party, the National Women's Party. Led by Carrie Chapman Catt, NAWSA was focused on Catt's "Winning Plan" of changing suffrage laws state by state. The leaders of the new party, Alice Paul and Lucy Burns, wanted to keep the pressure on Washington for a federal amendment. Just as the Republican Party had failed women's suffrage during reconstruction, so the Democratic Party had failed women during President Woodrow Wilson's first term.

"The dominant political party—the Democratic Party—has the power to liberate the women of the United States, but they have refused to exercise that power on our behalf, and on behalf of justice and of freedom. They have refused to put the party machinery back of the constitutional amendment," Inez declared in her speech.

During Wilson's first term, the Democratic Party controlled it all—the House of Representatives and the U.S. Senate as well as the presidency. While claiming to personally support suffrage, President Wilson had hidden behind the veil of his party and refused to put any pressure on Congress to pass an amendment.

"They have blocked the amendment at every turn. The Democratic leaders in the Senate forced it to defeat through a premature vote. In the House they have buried it in committee. Fourteen times the President has refused his help," Inez explained in her speech. "Therefore, women of the West, let no free woman, let no woman that respects herself and womankind, lend her strength to the Democratic party that turns away its face from justice to the women of the nation."

During the 1914 midterms, women voters in the west voted out twenty-four of forty-three Democratic members of Congress. Yet, they still had not succeeded in getting the House of Representatives to pass the Susan B. Anthony amendment. Likewise, President Wilson claimed to support a state-by-state approach to women's suffrage while his opponent for president, Republican Charles Evans Hughes, supported a federal amendment for women winning the vote. The National Women's Party decided to implement the same strategy in the 1916 presidential election by using political warfare to hold the party in power responsible.

"Now, for the first time in our history, women have the power to enforce their demands, and the weapon with which to fight for woman's liberation. You, women of the West, who possess that power, will you use it on behalf of women? We have waited so long and so patiently and so hopelessly for help from other political sources. May we not depend upon the co-operation and goodwill of women in politics?" Inez asked in her speech.

"Women of the West, stand by us now. Visit your displeasure upon that political party that has ignored and held cheaply the interests of women. Let no party, whatsoever its name, dare to slur the demands of women, as the Democratic Party has done, and come to you for your endorsement at the polls. Make them feel your indignation."

She upheld her belief in the timing of their strategy. "Liberty must be fought for. And, women of the nation, this is the time to fight. This is the time to demonstrate our sisterhood, our spirit, our blithe courage, and our will. It is women for women now, and shall be till the fight is won," she said multiple times, starting in Chicago on October 3, 1916. From there Inez traveled by train, making regular stops where she would speak at planned events, as well as multiple whistle stops, where she'd speak from the train platform.

"Sisters of the West, may we count on you? Think well before you answer. Other considerations press upon you. But surely this great question of woman's liberty comes first. How can our nation be free with half of its citizens politically enslaved? How can the questions that come before a government for decision, be decided aright, while half the people whom these decisions affect are mute?" she asked over and over again. From Chicago, her train took her to speak to the women of Wyoming, Idaho, Oregon, Washington, Montana, Utah, Nevada, and California.

"Women of the West, stand by us in this crisis. Give us your help and we shall win. Fight on our side and liberty is for all of us. For the first time in the world women are asked to unite with women in a common cause. Will you stand by?" she asked as she traveled through the high altitudes of America's western mountains.

"The gods of government help those who help themselves. Therefore, women and sisters, and one day fellow voters, let us help ourselves," she said. Irony undergirded her devotion to suffrage. "Most beautiful woman in US will be a guest," the *Topeka Journal* ran as a headline on October 2, 1916. In this article announcing the itinerary and campaign, the reporter noted that Inez was no longer a U.S. citizen. How? "Miss Milholland, when she married Eugene Boissevain, a citizen of The Netherlands, lost her American citizenship. This law applies only to American women, not to American men taking foreign wives." If women won the right to vote through a federal amendment, she would still be barred from voting as long as she was married to Boissevain. She wasn't swayed.

"Say to the rulers of this nation: 'You deal negligently with the interests of women at your peril. As you have sowed so shall ye reap,'" she boldly proclaimed.

"We, as women, refuse to uphold that party that has betrayed us. We refuse to uphold any party until all women are free. We are tired of being the political auxiliaries of men. It is the woman's fight only we are making. Together we shall stand, shoulder to shoulder for the greatest principle the world has ever known – the right of self-government," she declared, believing that the 1916 election would lead to a turning point.

The turning point for Inez, however, took place in Los Angeles, when she collapsed on stage in late October. She never made it to Arizona, Colorado, or Kansas. Instead, she found herself in a Los Angeles hospital.

"Mrs. Boissevain was stricken suddenly while addressing an audience in this city [Los Angeles] in the recent political campaign and fainted on the platform at the meeting," the press reported. Diagnosed with anemia, she'd been fighting symptoms of fatigue since mid September. Speaking multiple times a day would exhaust anyone, much less someone battling pernicious anemia, which today is known as vitamin B12 deficiency. Because traveling to high-altitude locations is not advised for patients with severe anemia, Inez's journey had made her condition worse.

"We have no money, no elaborate organization, no one interested in our success, except anxious-hearted women all over the country who cannot come to the battle line themselves," she said. Women in Arizona, Nevada, and Kansas would never hear her stump speech or these words: "Here and there in farm house and factory, by the fireside, in the hospital, and school-room, wherever women are sorrowing and working and hoping, they are praying for our success. Only the hopes of women have we; and our own spirit and a mighty principle."

Inez's spirit fought in that Los Angeles hospital. Receiving two blood transfusions from her sister revived her but only for a brief time. The National Women's Party had published her speech in mid October 1916 in the *Suffragist*.

"Women of these states, unite. We have only our chains to lose, and a whole nation to gain. Will you join us by voting against President Wilson and the Democratic candidates for Congress?" she asked in her speech over and over again.

Inez had exhausted herself through speaking multiple times a day, often declaring, "It is only for a little while. Soon the fight will be over. Victory is in sight."

"Noted suffrage worker is dead," Washington D.C.'s *Evening Star* reported on November 27, 1916. "Mrs. Inez Mulholland Boissevain succumbs to anemia in Los Angeles."

Newspapers throughout the nation published her obituary. The *Trenton Evening Times* made this tribute on November 27, 1916. "In 8 years her remarkable energies made her a famous American," the press declared, noting that she had been only thirty years old. "Perhaps there never was a girl who did so many things, attracted so much attention, was accorded so much space in the newspapers in the brief space of 8 years as she."

The Washington, D.C., press published the reaction of the National Women's Party. "Mrs. Boissevain is held by associates as martyr to the suffrage cause." The party leaders sent telegrams to her family. "It is a loss to all American women into our country. It is one more sorrowful instance of the waste of life and genius to this bitter fight of women for freedom. Women will consecrate themselves with new devotion to the cause." Remembering Inez's resilience, this new devotion showed the power of creative problem-solving.

Washington Suffrage Parade, March 3, 1913
(Library of Congress)

Washington Women's Suffrage Parade
(Library of Congress)

Inez Milholland as the herald for the 1913 Washington
Women's Suffrage Parade (Library of Congress)

Women's Suffrage Parade, Washington, D.C., 1913
(Library of Congress)

The Women's Suffrage parade began at the U.S.
Capitol, March 3, 1913 (Library of Congress)

The parade ended at the U.S. Treasury Building, where
they presented scenes in tableaux. Hedwiga Reicher
portrays Columbia, the female personification of
America. (Library of Congress)

Aviator Terah "T.T." Maroney & Lucy Burns fly over
Seattle, Washington, 1916 (Library of Congress)

9
COURAGEOUS CREATIVITY

When did the suffrage movement peak? The campaign reached its highest point in a literal way during the first week of October in 1916. Through the latest cutting-edge technology, "Lucy Burns the suffragist took a unique way of aiding the cause in Seattle. She went up in the air with a pilot in an aeroplane."[9] Portland's *Oregonian* newspaper published a photo of a smiling Lucy Burns and flying ace Lieutenant T.T. Maroney on October 8, 1916."

Peaking at a height of fourteen-hundred feet, Lucy flew with Maroney in an uncovered cockpit in a plane that resembled the one the Wright brothers first had flown thirteen years earlier. The thirty-eight-year-old described suffrage as reaching "the height of its career" as she scattered leaflets over Seattle from

---

[9] *Oregonian,* October 8, 1916. See page 199 for this chapter's endnotes.

the air. What the black-and-white photo couldn't show was her bright-red hair, which was piled high in layers as she sat in the unprotected open air. Her Irish red bun was a contrast to Seattle's gray skies. She looked like a red robin gliding through the clouds.

When the plane took off, she carried a promotional banner, but the rush of wind soon took it from her hands and carried it back to earth where it landed on a mill. According to the *Oregonian*, "The flight was entirely successful and it is likely that much attention was attracted to the movement of votes for women."

Like Inez Milholland, Lucy had traveled to the West for the 1916 campaign. She had focused her attention on Seattle as part of the National Women's Party effort to encourage western women to vote out members of the Democratic Party for failing to pass a federal suffrage amendment. Flying in an airplane was as novel as it was risky. Throwing leaflets out of it was a creative, out-of-the-box way to bring attention to their message. When conventional thinking fails, creative problem-solving enables leaders to find innovative solutions through fresh perspectives. Creativity is often needed to overcome obstacles. Sometimes it takes courage.

Little did Lucy realize on that day in 1916, when she felt on top of the world in Seattle, that within a year she would reach her life's darkest low and experience a night of horrors.

Two months later, the *Oregonian* featured Lucy in another story. This time the occasion was President Wilson's annual message to Congress, which is known today as the State of the Union address. Since Thomas Jefferson's presidency over a century earlier, presidents had submitted the message in writing. Wilson had broken with tradition by giving the message to Congress in person, which brought fresh attention to the otherwise stale address.

"President Wilson's address to Congress today was marked by a woman suffrage coup in the gallery," the *Oregonian* published on December 6, under the headline: "Suffrage banner flown in Capitol, coup executed as Wilson reads address." Wilson wasn't the only one to leverage the publicity surrounding his speech before both Houses of Congress.

"He was just about to begin a sentence 'the present laws governing the island in regulating the rights and privileges of its people are not just' when, over the rail of the gallery, where set a party of woman suffrage leaders, there fluttered down above the heads of an amazed assemblage of senators and representatives a second banner of suffrage yellow, bearing in great black letters the inscription; 'President Wilson, what will you do for woman suffrage?'"

Receiving a copy of Wilson's speech in advance, Lucy and the other suffragists present at the address unleashed the banner at the moment that the president asserted that men in the U.S. territory of Puerto Rico deserved the right to vote. By this time, Wilson personally supported women's suffrage and voted for it in a state referendum in New Jersey, his home state. The referendum failed, and he still refused to publicly back a federal amendment.

"As the banner rippled down, the suffragists sat smiling and unperturbed watching the effect." A teenage boy, known as a congressional page, took down the banner. How did Wilson respond?

"The president looked up, smiled broadly and without interruption continued reading." According to the *Oregonian*, the ladies had made their point, because the buzz after the speech was only about one thing: women voting. "Miss Lucy Burns declared the suffrage question was the only one before Congress today when President Wilson finished reading his address." Though not a literal coup, the banner had served its purpose of garnering attention.

"When he finished the Senators and representatives on the floor turned toward us and muttered the one word 'suffragist," Lucy said. "We feel we did our duty today and we never should have forgiven ourselves had we overlooked it."

Inez Milholland's death in late November 1916 hit Lucy and the other NWP members hard. Within a month, they had decided to hold a memorial for Inez at the U.S. Capitol on Christmas Day. The service attracted huge crowds. Then, on January 9, 1917, three-hundred women called on President Woodrow Wilson, who'd won re-election, to present Inez's memorial to him.

"The death of this lovely and brave woman symbolizes the whole daily sacrifice that vast numbers of women have made and our making for the sake of political freedom," the women read in a memorial to Inez. "We ask you with all the fervor and earnestness of our souls to exert your power over Congress and behalf of the national enfranchisement of women."

How did Wilson respond? Surely he would understand that the death of Inez brought fresh urgency to the cause? She may not have died on a battlefield at the hands of a gun or cannon, but she'd been a soldier in a political battle nonetheless. Now that he'd won reelection, surely he would be more open to pressuring the House of Representatives and the Senate for a federal amendment for women's suffrage? Surely he would recognize that his party had continued to lose seats in the House since the suffragists began holding the Democrats accountable?

When Wilson first became president, the Democrats held the majority in the House with 289 seats but had lost seventy-six seats since, lowering their total to 213 seats in 1917. House Republicans had 216 seats. The problem for both parties was the independents. Four independents caucused with the Democrats and one caucused with Republicans, giving them a tie of 217 votes each. Surely Wilson understood that his party would be on the verge of losing the House if women didn't get the right to vote? The dynamics in the Senate were more favorable to the president with the Democrats holding 54 seats and the Republicans holding 42.

"It is impossible for me until the orders of my party are

changed to do anything other than I am doing as a party leader. In this country, as in every other self-governing country, it is really through the instrumentality of parties that things can be accomplished," Wilson told the three-hundred women facing him at the memorial. "They are not accomplished by the individual voice but by concerted action, and that action must come only so fast as you can concert it. I have done my best and continue to do my best in the interest of a cause in which I personally believe."

Nothing but dead silence filled the room. Wilson abruptly left. As they returned back to their headquarters, which was across Pennsylvania Avenue on Lafayette Square, the women experienced a mix of emotions. Anger, hurt, and deep disappointment filled their hearts as they entered Cameron House at 21 Madison Place. The house had been known as the Little White House for its use over the years by vice presidents and other leading figures in Washington. The NWP had converted it into an operations center. Though disappointed with Wilson's response to Inez's memorial, they weren't surprised.

"We have gone to Congress. We have gone to the president during the last four years with great deputations, with small deputations. We have shown the interest all over the country in self-government for women," Harriet Stanton Blatch, daughter of Elizabeth Cady Stanton, addressed the women.

"Yet he tells us today that it is up to us to convert his party. Why? Never before did the Democratic party lie in the hands of one man as it lies today in the hands of President Wilson. He controls his party," she declared. "Yet he is not willing to lay a finger's weight on his party today for half the people of the United States." Blatch expressed her frustration at his desire for them to wait longer. Hadn't they put their all into their campaigns? They couldn't organize bigger or more influential meetings or parades. It was time for a change.

"We have to take a new departure. We have got to keep the question before him all the time. We have got to begin and begin immediately," she declared. "We have got to bring to the president, individually, day by day, week in and week out, the idea that great numbers of women want to be free, will be free, and want to know what he's going to do about it."

Then her words became personal, a call to action. "Won't you come and join us in standing day after day at the gates of the White House with banners asking, 'What will you do, Mr. President, for one-half the people of this nation?' Stand there as sentinels—sentinels of liberty, sentinels of self-government, Silent Sentinels."

Lucy couldn't have agreed more. A fellow suffragist described the light-eyed, fresh-complexioned Lucy as a figure "heroically sculptured, from marble." Lucy's strong, muscular, tall frame was a contrast to the delicate, demure-looking Alice Paul, NWP's chair, whose power came from her quiet but steely reserve. Both women were courageous and used their talents differently.

While Alice was the confident mastermind, Lucy was the diplomat. Both tapped the power of creativity to solve problems and bring fresh attention to the right for women to vote. Both fulfilled what Abigail Adams had politically prophesied when she wrote her husband John Adams in in 1776: "If particular care and attention is not paid to the ladies, we are determined to foment a rebellion, and will not hold ourselves bound by any laws in which we have no voice, or representation." Not enough care had been taken for enough women. More than twenty million women were governed without their consent and were unable to vote. One hundred and forty-one years later, in January 1917, Abigail's predicted rebellion was taking flight in a new, creative way.

"It fell to Lucy Burns, vice chairman of the organization, to be the leader of the new protest. Miss Burns is in appearance the very symbol of woman in revolt. Her abundant and glorious red hair burns and is not consumed—a flaming torch. Her body is strong and vital," a fellow suffragist later described Lucy, noting that her hair was full of sparkle, matching her temperament.

With a quick and warm personality, Lucy gave concise and clear speeches and instructions that motivated others. She "has a mental poise that is almost unsusceptible to fear." Her courageous creativity would be on display in ways Washington had never before witnessed.

Before the night ended, Lucy or one of the other party leaders had made a call or sent a telegram. Who received it? A reporter for the *Associated Press*.

Alaskans, who lived in a U.S. territory at the time, had the news before the suffragists revealed their first creative salvo. When readers opened the *Daily Alaska Dispatch* the morning after the memorial for Inez Milholland, they saw this headline: "Women are after Wilson for suffrage."

"The women's suffrage leaders, after another futile appeal to President Wilson for his support of the Anthony suffrage amendment legislation, announce that they will retaliate by picketing the White House with Silent Sentinels," the *Associated Press* article continued below. While Alaskans devoured this news around 6:00 a.m. Alaska Standard Time, Lucy and the NWP implemented their first demonstration.

At 10:00 a.m. Eastern Standard Time, twelve women wearing purple-gold-and-white sashes walked across the street and stood at the White House gate. Without saying a word, they held a banner that boldly declared:

"Mr. President, what will you do for woman suffrage? How long must women wait for liberty?" These were the last words that Inez had said publicly before she fainted three months earlier. Did Wilson try to stop them?

"White House officials said nothing would be done about it so long as the women created no disturbance nor attempted to enter the White House," Cleveland's *Plain Dealer* reported the next day under the headline, "Suffrage pickets flaunt banners at

White House." "The White House police stood smilingly by as the women took their post on the sidewalk just outside the entrance."

Lucy and the suffrage leaders announced that the Silent Sentinels would stand between 10:00 a.m. and 6:00 p.m. each day, rotating duty every three hours. "The announced purpose of the picketing is to make it impossible for President Wilson to enter or leave the White House without being confronted with reminders of the suffrage cause."

Seemingly amused at first, President Wilson smiled at them as he passed by in the early days of the picketing. To his surprise, day after day women silently stood holding banners in the rain, sleet, and snow. From young to old, women came from every state in the union. Their creativity continued. Lucy and Alice organized special days for the pickets, such as college day, teacher day, labor day, and professional day, with women physicians, to show the depth of women's capabilities and progress and the breadth of who needed the vote. Just as they'd shown in the 1913 parade in Washington, D.C., so they declared their united goal through this banner in January 1917: "We demand an amendment to the Constitution of the United States enfranchising women."

How far would the picketing go? Would it continue after President Wilson declared war against Germany's Kaiser Wilhelm in April 1917, which brought the United States into World War I? Women suffragists had listened to promises that if they put aside their goal of voting during the Civil War, they would be rewarded after it ended. They hadn't been. Alice and Lucy wouldn't make the same mistake. After all, wasn't President Wilson requiring mothers to send their sons to Europe in the name of democracy? Shouldn't those mothers have a say in their government?

The pickets continued. By June, six months had passed since the pickets had begun, and Congress had not taken action on the Susan B. Anthony amendment. The longer the Senate and House waited to vote on the amendment, the more creative the sentinel campaign became. They soon discovered something that can sometimes happen when thinking outside the box goes so far that it breaks the box. It was one thing to make a case for civil rights during a war. It was another to protest in a way that impugned others involved.

"Cries of 'traitor' and 'treason' were sounded," one newspaper reported on June 21, 1917. "Screaming 'traitors!'" another described. "You are a dirty yellow traitor!" a woman shrieked at Lucy Burns and Mrs. Lawrence Lewis. The headlines proclaimed: "Banners of Silent Sentinels torn down by angry mob."

Originally from Brooklyn, New York, Lucy's hometown newspaper, the *Sun and New York Press* covered the story in detail. "Bearing their banner aloft, the two women marched from the headquarters of the woman's party to the west gate on Pennsylvania Avenue shortly after noon, just before the Russian visitors were due to arrive."

After declaring America's entry into World War I, Wilson spent the next few weeks ramping up America's war machine. Among the myriad details involved was coordinating with U.S. allies, such as France, England, and Russia. The year 1917 had started with revolution in Russia. In February 1917, the people of Russia overthrew their czar, ending centuries of imperial rule. While American leaders thought democracy would take root in Russia, they did not know that the Bolsheviks would take power in November 1917 then murder the Russian czar and his family and turn Russia into a Soviet empire. When Russian diplomats visited President Wilson on June 21, 1917, Americans incorrectly viewed Russia as an emerging free nation, reminiscent of America's revolution in 1776.

When the diplomats met with Wilson and Secretary of State Elihu Root at the White House, Lucy Burns and another sentinel held up this banner: "To the Russian Envoys, President

Wilson and Envoy Root are deceiving Russia when they say 'We are a democracy, help us win the world war so that democracy may survive.'"

But that wasn't all. "We the women of America tell you that America is not a democracy. Twenty-million American women are denied the right to vote. President Wilson is the chief opponent of their national enfranchisement," the banner read. "Help us make this nation really free. Tell our government it must liberate its people before it can claim free Russia as an ally."

Three hundred people gathered around the sentinels. Like all throngs, this curious crowd had its share of hoodlums and ruffians. "It's an outrage. It's treasonable," were among the cries. Some were angry because their sons were among the American servicemen headed to Europe. They saw the banner as a slight against America's soldiers rather than as an expression of free speech. One person tore the banner from its frame.

"Miss Burns and Mrs. Lewis stuck to their post holding the bare wooden framework between them. They faced the crowd without flinching."

Not only that but a policeman also intervened. "The police obtained torn sections of the banner and took it into the White House office." How did the White House respond? The chief of staff made it clear to the chief of police not to arrest the women.

How did Lucy react? She and Mrs. Lewis returned to their headquarters. "The two banner bearers, their lips tightly compressed then marched with the framework of the banner, bearing a few tatted shreds, along the avenue to the headquarters on Lafayette Square, followed by a small crowd that jeered and hooted them."

Some thought the banner violated the Logan Act, a 1799 act that prohibited U.S. citizens from corresponding with foreign governments without permission from the United States. Although one person had been indicted under it, no one had ever been convicted. What foreign government were they supposedly corresponding with? Russia? Germany? Neither. They weren't coordinating with any foreign power.

"The National Woman's Party remains strong for the White House pickets and hot against Envoy Root. Their ardor is not cooled in the least by the mobbing of Miss Lucy Burns and Mrs. Lawrence Lewis of yesterday.

Opinion writers chastised the women for "a deplorable lack of propriety and good judgment." Still others accused the National Woman's Party of having gone too far. The strongest criticism came from their competitors.

"Dr. Anna Howard Shaw, honorary president of the National Woman Suffrage Association, issued a statement characterizing the picketing of the White House as 'the greatest obstacle now existing to the passage of the federal woman suffrage amendment in Congress.'" Dr. Shaw also disagreed with their assertion about Wilson. She said, "That the president is the chief opponent to the national enfranchisement of women is not true. President Wilson has done more for enfranchising women in this country than all other presidents put together. He has assisted us in many ways which have won the gratitude of the National Suffrage Association."

What was the strategy of NAWSA's Carrie Chapman Catt and Dr. Shaw at this time? While the NWP, also referred to as the Congressional Union, picketed in Washington, Catt and Shaw were steering a campaign in New York to give women the vote. Catt's winning plan, as she called it, focused on detailed organizing in the states. If a federal amendment passed, she could tap her organizational groundwork in the states for the ratification phase.

While the Big Apple was the apple of Catt's eye during the summer of 1917, her approach to President Wilson was more deferential. She thought Congress was the problem. Because neither the Democrats nor the Republicans had a two-thirds majority in either chamber of Congress, Catt had concluded that a federal amendment was unlikely. Neither party wanted the other to get credit for passing it. Whichever party did receive the credit would reap the reward of the women's collective vote in the next election. It was hard for Republicans to join Democrats when the Democrats would get the credit and vice versa. Catt had concluded that Wilson wasn't the main obstacle; party rivalry was.

In contrast, Lucy had long held Wilson responsible for the failure to grant all women the right to vote, as she'd publicly stated. "For the President of the United States, who incorporates in himself the power of the whole nation, and who is, therefore, more responsible than any other person today for the subjugation of women, to declare that he washes his hands of their whole case, is to presume upon greater ignorance among women than he will find they possess," Lucy had written in *The Suffragist*. "Nevertheless, we are specifically informed by the President that it is 'not proper' for us to 'cross-examine' him on the grounds of his refusal to help us. Only fitfully do women realize the astounding arrogance of their rulers."

However, the chief of police in Washington, D.C., Major Raymond Pullman warned the NWP that law-enforcement officers soon would begin arresting the picketers. Perhaps their banners had become too sensational. How could they solve this problem? How could they continue to be provocative without insulting those in the military? They found a solution in President Woodrow Wilson's Flag Day speech. Wilson had declared June 14, the day the Continental Congress had adopted the first U.S. flag in 1777, as Flag Day. In strong terms, he'd given a speech outlining Germany's transgressions, such as spying, U-boat warfare, and the Kaiser's attempt to make Mexico an ally of Germany to threaten the United States.

Armed with their attorney's assurance that they had a legal right to protest, Lucy and Katherine Morey carried their most creative, most clever sign to date. "We shall fight for the things we have always held nearest our hearts, for democracy, for the right of those who submit to authority to have a voice in their own government." Why was this both creative and sly? The statement was Wilson's own, from his recent Flag Day speech. Yet despite holding banners featuring nothing but the president's words, not theirs, they were arrested. At the police station, the officers couldn't initially identify their crime. Finally, they decided to charged Lucy and Katherine with obstructing traffic, before releasing them.

And so the pattern began. Picket. Arrest. Release. Picket. Arrest. Jail.

Undeterred, they continued to picket. Though they toned down the heat of their messages for a time, they held fast to their just goal of giving women the right to vote. On July 4, the Silent Sentinels tapped the sentiment of the Declaration of Independence. "Governments derive their just powers from the consent of the governed." With France as an ally, they celebrated Bastille Day with banners that said, "Liberty, equality, fraternity."

How did the police respond? They arrested sixteen women for the Bastille Day protest and, after a trial, sentenced them to two months to the Occoquan Workhouse.

Watching in the courtroom that day was Dudley Field Malone, an attorney who had been appointed by President Wilson to be customs collector of New York. Malone was so shocked at the length of the sentences that he immediately contacted the White House and set up a meeting with President Wilson. A longtime political supporter and fundraiser, Malone was an ardent supporter of the president's. He'd campaigned for him in 1912 and then again in 1916.

In his substantive meeting with President Wilson, expressed his concern over several issues related to the jailed picketers. "The manhandling of the women by the police was outrageous and the entire trial (before a judge of your own appointment) was a perversion of justice," Malone told Wilson.

How did Wilson respond to Malone standing against the

poor treatment the women received during their arrest? "If the situation is as you describe it, it is shocking," said the president.

"Although we might not agree with the 'manners' of picketing, citizens had a right to petition the president," Malone told Wilson.

Malone also relayed to Wilson that people were aware of the behind-the-scenes coordination between the president's staff and the D.C. commissioners who oversaw the D.C. police. Wilson's own secretary and another cabinet member had discussed what to do about the Silent Sentinels with the D.C. commissioners. Wilson claimed that he wasn't aware of this coordination.

Believing that women's suffrage was a necessary part of America's program for world democracy, Malone asked the president to make suffrage an urgent war measure in Congress. Wilson's reply saddened Malone as much as it shocked him.

"The enfranchisement of women is not at all necessary to a program of democracy and I see nothing in the argument that it is a war measure unless you mean that American women will not loyally support the war unless they are given the vote."

Countering that women would support the war without the vote, Malone tried to appeal to Wilson's sense of justice.

"Mr. President, if you, as the leader, will persuade the administration to pass the federal Amendment you will release from the suffrage fight the energies of thousands of women which will be given with redoubled zeal to the support of your program for international justice."

While Wilson refused to make the Susan B. Anthony amendment a war measure, after his meeting with Malone he took some significant action. What did he do? He pardoned the sixteen women arrested on Bastille Day. They would not have to serve two months at the Occoquan prison.

One of the women came up with an idea. Perhaps they'd

heard about the president's conversation with Malone. His inability to see the injustice of denying them the vote, especially during war, infuriated them. Knowing that members of Congress had called Wilson names behind his back, the Silent Sentinels created the most provocative banner of their campaign. Would they dare? Should they dare? They dared, making dozens of banners. The headlines told it all; they had gone too far for some in the military.

"Shoot at 'suffs' for their insults," the *Trenton Evening Times* declared on August 15, 1917. "For two hours yesterday afternoon 2,000 excited citizens, led by soldiers, sailors, and marines, besieged Cameron house, the headquarters of the national women's party, while one policeman wondered uneasily in and out of the crowd."

A little after 4:00 p.m., a woman from Richmond, Virginia, left NWP headquarters and walked toward the White House. She carried a banner: "Kaiser Wilson, Have you forgotten how you sympathized with the poor Germans that were not self-governed? 20,000,000 American women are not self-governed. Take the beam out of your own eye."

Someone in the crowd ripped it from her before she made it to the White House. Another suffragist carried another banner with the same inscription. One after the other tried to carry the message until they realized it was futile to try to reach the White House. Instead, Lucy led the women to the balcony to display the banners.

Outraged at this insult to their commander in chief, the soldiers, sailors, and marines led the crowd in fighting back. Chaos broke out. They threw eggs and tomatoes at the windows and doors of NWP headquarters and at the women. Someone placed a long ladder against the house. When a telegraph operator at the Navy Department saw Lucy Burns with the Kaiser Wilson banner, he shimmied up the ladder. "Miss Lucy Burns appeared on the balcony and held a Kaiser Wilson banner between the American flag and the great purple, white and gold banner that has floated for two years over Cameron house." He ripped the banner from Lucy. "But for Miss Burns' superb strength she would have been dragged over the railing of the balcony to be plunged to the ground. The mob watched with fascination while she swayed to and fro and wrestled with two young sailors. And still no attempt by the police to quell the riot," Silent Sentinel Doris Stevens reflected.

The eggs and tomatoes had their desired effect, "striking at the women until they were forced back into the house and threw the flags onto the ground." With no more pickets left on the street, the women fought back by bringing out more banners and holding them up to the doors and windows and a "shower of missiles began again."

With a clenched fist, one sailor struck a woman in the face. "Why did you do that?" she asked. Pausing for a moment in bewilderment, the man replied that he didn't know. "A sailor with a pistol in his hand joined the crowd in Lafayette Park, directly opposite the house, and a moment later a bullet shattered the glass in the large bow window on the second floor of the house a few inches above the heads of two women who were watching. The bullet embedded in the ceiling," the *Trenton Evening Times* reported. At the end of two hours, thirty-six banners had been ripped into shreds. Of those, twenty-seven were Kaiser Wilson banners. Though the man who hit the woman in the face and the man who fired the pistol weren't arrested, one mob member was arrested for desecrating the U.S. flag after pulling it down from the women's headquarters.

Decades later, a woman who worked for a U.S. president captured the importance of logic in messaging, which the suffragists excelled at. "The most moving thing in a speech is its logic. It's not the flowery words or flourishes, it's not the sentimental exhortations, it's never the faux poetry we're all subjected to these days," President Ronald Reagan's speechwriter Peggy Noonan wrote in a book about the art of communication. "It's the logic behind your case. A good case well-argued and well-said is inherently moving," she explained. Why does logic stick with people? Noonan had an answer. "It shows respect for the brains of the listeners. There is an implicit compliment in it. It shows you're a serious person and understand that you are talking to other serious people."

Regardless of whether some thought the women went too far in the summer of 1917, they showed courageous creativity. They were thinking out of the box to solve the problem of women's denial from the ballot box. The logic behind the Silent Sentinel banners stands the test of time.

Their most effective, most long-lasting messages were the ones that were clever, that revealed universal truths without name-calling, such as using Wilson's own words against him. If the first phase was one of courageous creativity, the next phase required creative courage, where the creativity became the adjective describing the courage. The life and health of the women depended on it.

The riot, as well as the scathing backlash in the press against the Kaiser Wilson banners, illustrates Noonan's point. While it garnered attention, the depiction of Wilson as Kaiser went too far for the crowd, though it didn't justify the mob's violence or the punishment they later received. Was the president doing enough to pressure Congress for women's suffrage? No. But did that equate him with America's number-one enemy, the German Kaiser provoking World War I? No. Though their courageous creativity had included many logical messages, ones that were well-stated and well-argued, their Kaiser Wilson banner had gone too far for many Americans. Some claimed they were doing more harm than good for the cause of votes for women.

An editorialist in the *Chicago Evening Post* issued one of the strongest rebukes, which the *Daily Gate City* and *Constitution Democrat* of Keokuk, Iowa, reprinted on August 24, 1917. Under the headline "Lucy Burns' Battalion of Death," the article targeted Lucy above all of the Silent Sentinels.

"That restless egotist Miss Lucy Burns of the Congressional

Union (also known as the NWP) ought to be supremely happy now," he said, referring to the Congressional Union, the D.C. lobbying arm that Alice Paul and Lucy had previously led for Carrie Chapman Catt's National American Woman's Suffrage Association. "In her 'Kaiser Wilson' she has found something so unpatriotic and insulting that indignant Americans actually do something about it."

This editorialist criticized their strategy of leveraging press attention for their cause. "Thus there is manufactured a continuous supply of sensational publicity. Lack of this since Miss Burns' ridiculous failure to 'defeat Wilson with 4 million women's votes' almost starved and disrupted her autocratic union." He wasn't giving her enough credit. Though Wilson had won reelection in 1916, his Electoral College victory was significantly lower than it had been in 1912, when he received a whopping 435 Electoral College votes. In 1916, President Wilson had received 277 Electoral College votes while his opponent, Republican Charles Evans Hughes, had garnered 254. Though many factors and issues were at play in that election, from the suffragist viewpoint, Hughes had supported the Susan B. Anthony amendment. Nonetheless, this editorialist skewered Lucy for the failure.

"Even picketing couldn't revive it. Death from quiet ridicule seemed in sight. Then Miss Burns, being an efficient press agent, bethought herself of the publicity values that lay in insulting the ambassadors of America's allies and the president himself. She is succeeding magnificently in this plan of action," this opinion writer continued, noting that money and recruits were pouring into their headquarters. "All is well with the Congressional Union (if you omit its soul). No munition maker has capitalized the war more effectively than has Miss Burns," he wrote. He then compared her to an unethical, mob-friendly mayor of Chicago.

"Yet the sinister fact lies underneath it. Miss Lucy Burns' Congressional Union is killing its ostensible cause. It is the 'Battalion of death' for the cause of woman suffrage in

America."

Though he was correct that they had used sensationalism to attract press coverage, he overlooked the strong logic behind their banners and missed their real motivations. Neither Lucy nor Alice was self-absorbed or self-seeking. They'd met a few years earlier when they'd traveled separately to England to assist in the suffragette movement there. Under the leadership of Emmeline Pankhurst, suffragettes in England had founded the Women's Social and Political Union that engaged in militant tactics, including window smashing and police confrontation. Though the group received criticism for its later use of arson, Pankhurst had ordered her members to desist and support the war effort when World War I began in 1914.

When Alice and Lucy had been imprisoned together in England, Alice had noticed Lucy's U.S. flag pin on her lapel at the police station. The pair became friends and concluded that violence would not work in achieving suffrage in America. Some compared their working partnership to that of Susan B. Anthony and Elizabeth Cady Stanton in the previous century. Their press strategy wasn't about ego or self-promotion. They weren't making sensational banners to draw attention to their names or reputations. Both originated from faith backgrounds that taught humility. Lucy was a devoted Catholic and Alice was an equality-driven Quaker.

They demonstrated courageous creativity for one thing only: suffrage. Once, when a woman volunteer became miffed that Alice had not thanked her for her work, Alice responded that the work wasn't for her but for suffrage. It wasn't her place to thank her. After that, however, Alice tried to show volunteers gratitude more often.

National Woman's Party members later reflected on these criticisms against their picketing. "We have been told there is a deep disgrace resting upon the origin of this nation. The nation originated in the sharpest sort of criticism of public policy. We originated, to put it in the vernacular, in a kick, and if it be unpatriotic to kick, why then the grown man is unlike the child," NWP officer Doris Stevens recalled.

They believed that their protest was similar to the protests against King George III during the American Revolution. Back then, men had thrown tea overboard and agitated by tarring and feathering British officials. They'd hung effigies of tax collectors in town squares. They'd refused to comply with taxes, such as the Stamp Act, and had embraced new doctrines, such as no taxation without representation and the idea that their rights came from God, not government.

"We have forgotten the very principle of our origin if we have forgotten how to object, how to resist, how to agitate, how to pull down and build up, even to the extent of revolutionary practices, if it be necessary to readjust matters."

Keenly aware of the fallout from the riot on August 10, Alice and Lucy decided to set aside the Kaiser Wilson banners and chose ones whose logic was hard to ignore. They also spoke to the context of women's plight during World War I. Despite this more measured tone, days later, on August 18, six women were arrested because they held these flags: "Mr. President, how long must women be denied a voice in a government which is conscripting their sons?" Another one featured this message: "The government orders our banners destroyed because they tell the truth."

On August 29, 1917, Pennsylvania's *Wilkes-Barre Times Leader* summed up what had happened over the course of ten days. "50 arrested." Lucy Burns was arrested on August 28 with nine others in front of the White House. Arrested in groups, many including Lucy were out on bail. Seventeen were scheduled to go to the D.C. district jail, and twenty-two were supposed to go to the Occoquan Workhouse in Lorton, Virginia, if they lost their appeal. Was Lucy ready to give up? "Her convictions are all vigorous and I do not think Lucy Burns would hesitate for a moment to suffer torture, to die, for them," a colleague observed. Were these words prophetic?

Lucy Burns, 1917 (Library of Congress)

The Lucy Burns Museum is located at the Workhouse
Arts Center, the former Occoquan prison in
Lorton, Virginia.

Silent Sentinels picket at the White House,
1917 (Library of Congress)

Women from New York picket at the White House,
1917 (Library of Congress)

Alice Paul, 1920 (Library of Congress

Protesting arrests, 1917 (Library of Congress)

10
CREATIVE COURAGE &
THE NIGHT OF TERROR

Worms—not noodles—topped the soup at the Occoquan Workhouse, the Virginia prison where many of the Silent Sentinels had been sent. "When our friends were sent to prison, they expected the food would be extremely plain, but they also expected that . . . enough eatable food would be given them to maintain them in their ordinary state of health. This has not been the case,"[10] Lucy Burns wrote on August 30, 1917, to a D.C. commissioner about the conditions at the Occoquan Workhouse.

"The hominy, the chief article of the morning meal, sour and dirty. The meat served at the midday meal is very tough, old and often tainted. The cornbread served at dinner and supper cannot be eaten. One of the prisoners found worms in it. The soup served at dinner and supper is often very bad," she wrote, noting that soup and cornbread were the only food served at dinner. Sometimes prisoners chose not to eat rather than eat chicken-noodle-worm soup.

"The hygienic conditions have been improved at Occoquan

---

[10] Doris Stevens, *Jailed for Freedom*. See page 201 for this chapter's endnotes.

since a group of suffragists were imprisoned there. But they are still bad. The water they drink is kept in an open pail, from which it is ladled into a drinking cup. The prisoners frequently dip the drinking cup directly into the pail." It was unclear which was worse, the drinking water or the shower sanitation.

"The same piece of soap is used for every prisoner. As the prisoners in Occoquan are sometimes seriously afflicted with disease, this practice is appallingly negligent." Prisoners were allowed only one shower a week.

She also had received testimony of violent treatment of past prisoners, giving her reason to fear for the six women currently imprisoned there. "Concerning the general conditions of the person, I am enclosing with this letter, affidavit of Mrs. Virginia Bovee, an ex-officer of the workhouse," Lucy wrote. "The prisoners for whom I am counsel are aware that cruel practices go on at Occoquan. On one occasion they heard Superintendent Whittaker kicking a woman in the next room. They heard Whittaker's voice, the sound of blows, and the woman's cries."

When the arrests of the Silent Sentinels first began in late June, the police were unsure how to handle their charges. At first, they were arrested and released. The police thought that the arrests alone would stop the protests. They were mistaken.

Believing that they weren't breaking the law, the Silent Sentinels continued. The longer the pattern continued, the more stringent the punishment. Fines were applied. The ladies refused to pay them. They were sent to the D.C. district jail for three days, then six days. They hired an attorney to fight the charges and to defend their right to picket. Over time, two hundred and eighteen women were arrested, many repeatedly. When the D.C. jail became too crowded, more than seventy women were sent to the Occoquan Workhouse, a prison in Lorton, Virginia.

After her arrest on August 28, 1917, Lucy sensed that she was likely to lose her appeal and face a longer time in jail, either in D.C.'s district jail or the Occoquan Workhouse, which she'd recently visited to check on six suffragists imprisoned there.

While their picketing campaign had required courageous creativity, this next phase would call for something different. No longer could they hold a bold banner with a creative slogan to declare their message. They would need every ounce of courage to endure whatever awaited them in jail. Sensing this, Lucy made a critical decision in the window between her arrest on August 28 and the hearing for her appeal on September 4. Tapping some creative courage, she strategically wrote this letter about the prison conditions on August 30. She expected to enter into those conditions within days.

Despite knowing the jail's conditions, Lucy and a dozen others picketed in front of the White House on September 4, 1917. Mindful of the context of picketing during World War I and the accusations against them from many in the military, they took the point of view of the mothers of the doughboys going off to war. They stood silently at the White House with this simple message: "Mr. President, how long must women be denied a voice in the government that is conscripting their sons?"

Lucy and the others were sentenced to the Occoquan Workhouse for sixty days—the longest punishment yet enacted against them. Their imprisonment led to a bold decision from one of President Wilson's biggest boosters. Though his courage took a traditional form, it was eye-catching nonetheless.

"Dudley F. Malone resigns as customs collector at New York," the *Pueblo Chieftan* declared in its headline, along with hundreds of newspapers across the country. Other headlines gave the reason for his resignation in the story's lead. "Malone resigns as protest to Wilson" and "Malone quits as a protest against arrest of Suffs."

Some headlines were even more specific. His decision was not only about the arrests of the Silent Sentinels but also about the Susan B. Anthony amendment stalled in Congress. "Protest to Wilson against failure of President to support suffrage amendment."

One newspaper editor pointed out the personal cost of Malone's sacrifice. He wasn't just giving up any job. As the president's point man at New York's port, he was willingly relinquishing one of the highest prizes in the federal government, the position once held by President Chester Arthur. "Dudley Field Malone gives up best paying job in the government service because Wilson has failed to advocate passing a federal suffrage amendment." In the lead-up to World War I, Malone's position had been particularly important because of the danger that German U-boats had posed to passenger ships entering and departing New York. His job was a matter of national security.

South Dakota's *Aberdeen American* had made Malone's resignation its lead story. He'd shared something in common with Lucy Burns in the presidential election of 1916. Both had targeted the women voters in the West. Unlike Lucy, who'd called on those women to vote against Wilson and the Democratic Party for failing to take action on national suffrage, Malone had asked those women voters to give Wilson another chance to endorse a constitutional amendment and "felt obliged to resign and devote himself to redeeming that promise." The *Aberdeen American* published excerpts from Malone's resignation letter.

"Last autumn as the representative of your administration, I went into the woman suffrage states to urge your reelection," Malone wrote to President Wilson. "The most difficult argument to meet among the seven million women voters was the failure of the Democratic Party, through four years of power, to pass the federal suffrage amendment, looking toward the enfranchisement of all the women of the country."

California, which had given its electoral votes to former President Theodore Roosevelt in 1912, was pivotal. "The rest of those states, and principally in California, which ultimately decided the election by the votes of women, the women voters were urged to support you and your party, as the more likely way to enfranchise the rest of the women of the country," Malone pointed out. "And if the women of the west voted to re-elect you, I promised them I would spend all my energy, at any sacrifice to myself, who gets the present Democratic administration to pass the federal suffrage amendment."

Knowing that Wilson's men had influenced the D.C. commissioners in deciding what to do about the picketing, Malone hit Wilson hard about the latest round of sentences. "But the present policy of the administration, in permitting splendid American women to be sent to jail in Washington, not for carrying offensive banners nor for picketing, but on the technical charge of obstructing traffic, is the denial even of their constitutional right to petition for and demand the passage of the federal suffrage amendment. It therefore now becomes my profound obligation to actively keep my promise to the women of the West."

He used a shoe-on-the-other-foot argument. "And if the men of this country had been peacefully demanding for over half a century the political right or privilege to vote and had been continuously ignored or met with evasion by successive congresses, as have the women, you Mr. President, as a lover of liberty, would be the first to comprehend and forgive their inevitable impatience and righteous indignation." Knowing that World War I had consumed Wilson's presidency, Malone made his case for giving women the right to vote in the context of the current war.

"To me, Mr. President, this is not only a measure of justice and democracy, it is also an urgent war measure. The women of the nation are, and always will be, loyal to the country and the passage of the suffrage amendment is only the first step towards their national emancipation."

Knowing Wilson's background as a political science and history professor, Malone zeroed in on the injustice of disenfranchising women.

"But unless the government takes at least this first step

toward their enfranchisement, how can the government ask millions of American women, educated in our schools and colleges, and millions of American women, in our homes, or toiling for economic independence in every line of industry, to give up by conscription their men and happiness to a war for democracy in Europe, while these women citizens are denied the right to vote on the policies of the government which demands of them such sacrifice?" Malone sought to assure Wilson that his other backers would support him if he took the responsibility on this issue as leader of his party.

"For this reason, many of your most ardent friends and supporters feel that the passage of the federal suffrage amendment as a war measure which could appropriately be urged by you at this session of Congress."

Making a bold, courageous assertion, he added this authentic zinger: "It is true that this amendment would have to come from Congress, but the present Congress shows no earnest desire to enact this legislation for the simple reason that you, as the leader of the party in power, have not yet suggested it."

His criticism of the president continued unabashed, revealing his courage and willingness to speak truth to power. "For the whole country gladly acknowledges, Mr. President, that no vital piece of legislation has come through Congress these five years except by your extraordinary and brilliant leadership. And what millions of men and women today hope is that you will give the federal suffrage amendment to the women of the country by the valor of your leadership now. It will hearten the mothers of the nation, eliminate a just grievance, and turn the devoted energies of brilliant women to a more hearty support of the government in this crisis."

How did Wilson respond? Did he have the courage to change his mind and call on Congress to take up the Susan B. Anthony amendment? Did he pardon Lucy and the other prisoners? Did he respond to the merits and points of Malone's case? No. Instead he chose an anti-suffragist as the next leader of the port authority.

One person, however, had changed his mind. After visiting Lucy and the other prisoners at the Occoquan Workhouse on September 14, Senator Andrieus Jones, chairman of the Senate suffrage committee was so disturbed that he took swift action. The next day, he filed his committee's report and recommended that the full Senate pass the suffrage amendment. By a vote of 181 to 107, the House of Representatives also took action and voted to create a committee to take up the women's suffrage issue.

Still another lawmaker, Senator Lawrence Lewis, was so appalled by the conditions at Occoquan after visiting suffragists there that he launched an investigation of the conditions.

While the picketing and arrests continued on the outside, Lucy and several others launched a form of creative courage inside the prison. At first, they tried to improve the conditions for all prisoners, not just the suffragists. When this failed, they launched an effort to be treated as political prisoners. For her leadership, Lucy was removed to solitary confinement.

"As political prisoners we the undersigned, refuse to work," their letter to the prison board declared. "We have taken this stand as a matter of principle, after careful consideration, and from it we shall not recede."

They believed their sixty-day sentences were unjust because both the U.S. Constitution and the Clayton Act governing Washington, D.C., allowed for peaceful protests. "Conscious, therefore of having acted in accordance with the highest standards of citizenship, we ask the commissioners of the district to grant us the rights due political prisoners," they explained. "We ask exemption from prison work, that our legal right to consult counsel be recognized, to have food sent to us from outside, supply ourselves with writing material for as much correspondence as we may need, to receive books, letters, newspapers, our relatives and friends."

Angry that the prison guards had separated them, they asked permission to see each other and that "Miss Lucy Burns, who is in full sympathy with this letter, be released from solitary confinement in another building and given back to us."

How did the commissioners respond? Rather than recognize them as political prisoners, they threatened to place the women in solitary confinement. Not only that, but within days, the police also arrested Alice Paul. A judge sentenced her to seven months. Could they survive prison?

Was the news true? Was Lucy Burns running for Congress? If so, how could this be possible if she didn't have the right to vote?

"Militant suffs now nominate two for Congress," was the headline in Lucy's hometown paper, the *Sun and New York Press*, on November 14, 1917, including this subhead: "White House picketer and Bronx woman have eyes on the Capitol."

The article that followed didn't report a recent event. It made one up. "Scene: House of Representatives sometime early next year. Speaker drawls: the gentleman—ahem! That is to say the lady from New York," the reporter wrote, hypothesizing a future event. "Whereupon there arises from the seat of the Brooklyn Congresswoman, a young woman with flaming red hair." The vision featured Lucy occupying the seat.

Where was this news coming from? "That is what may happen if the National Woman's or pro-White House picket party persists in its intention, declared yesterday, of nominating Miss Lucy Burns to run for the seat in Congress made vacant by the election of Representative Daniel J. Griffin as sheriff of Kings County."

Although the rumor came from the NWP, it didn't originate from Washington, D.C., but its New York headquarters. Also weighing in was Lucy's sister, who told the reporter, "There is one thing certain. Nobody in this country knows more about Congress than Miss Burns does."

How was it possible for Lucy to run for Congress? Ten days earlier, on November 3, 1917, Lucy and the others were released from their sixty-day jail sentences. Three days after that, on November 6, New Yorkers made history by passing a referendum giving women in New York the right to vote. This meant that Lucy Burns could now vote in her home state.

"New York has now gone over the top for the whole world in this suffrage victory," NAWSA's Dr. Anna Howard Shaw declared.

"Twelve thousand women worked for their cause in the city during the balloting. There were joyful scenes, with hugs, kisses and real masculine back slapping at (NAWSA) suffrage headquarters when word came that the amendment was going through," the *Wilkes-Barre Times Leader* reported, while noting that the organization was worried about backlash from NWP's tactics. "The feared negative vote resulting from picketing operations at the White House failed to materialize."

What had made the difference this time? "President Wilson's support of the franchise in New York was believed to have been an important factor in the victory."

Within a week of Alice Paul's arrest, the president weighed in on the New York vote. "Wilson gives full support to suffrage, urges all states to extend franchise, personal and party wish."

Meeting with a hundred women from New York in the White House's east room, Wilson had blessed the referendum. Though "the president went further today than he has ever gone," he continued to emphasize his support for state, rather than federal, suffrage.

The news of women being able to vote in the next election and the empty congressional seat in Brooklyn led to the rumor of Lucy Burns running for Congress. The woman sharing the rumor with a reporter "admitted that the fact that Miss Burns probably will be sent to Occoquan workhouse for a term of anywhere from 7 months to a year when her case comes up next Friday is a drawback, as it is generally considered necessary for a candidate to be on hand to make a few speeches and so forth."

Ten days after her release from prison, Lucy returned to the picket line along with dozens of others on November 13. Angry over Alice Paul's imprisonment, they picketed the White House.

"Miss Lucy Burns of Brooklyn New York brought up the rear with a banner quoting the words of President Wilson: 'The time has come to conquer or submit. For us there is but one choice; we have made it.'"

Forty-one women from sixteen states were arrested in five groups for obstructing traffic. The judge sentenced them the next day. Just as Alice had received seven months, so Lucy received the longest term. Clearly the authorities were sending a message.

"Miss Lucy Burns denounced by the judge as the ring leader, was given, the sentence of 6 months. He said the whole history of picketing showed that the women were using the court and the sentence imposed on them to further suffrage."

At this Lucy interrupted. "Your honor, I object. We have been arrested, charged, found guilty and sentenced for obstructing traffic. You have no right now to mention picketing."

"You are a menace to the peace and order of the District of Columbia," he replied.

As Lucy left the courtroom, a reporter told her that she had been mentioned as a candidate to replace the outgoing congressman from Brooklyn. She couldn't have been more surprised.

"I wouldn't consider it for a moment. I have no illusions to enter Congress." Instead, she again demanded to be treated as a political prisoner once she reached the Occoquan Workhouse. What happened next would require her to muster every ounce of courage to survive. Would her creative ingenuity be enough to save her?

"Lucy Burns was made fast to bars, she says," was the headline in the *Sun* and *New York Press* three days later, on November 17. "Organization plans to take matter of punishment inflicted into court."

The sensational story spread across the nation. "Occoquan guard accused by suffragist inmate, who says prison keepers drag women and put them in room with men suffering from delirium," the *Denver Post* reported the same day, reporting the news that the guard "threatens to intern picket in sardine box with mustard on her."

How did the newspapers know what was going on? The daughter of the founder of the *Sun* and *New York Press* was imprisoned with Lucy. "Story of indignities smuggled from workhouse to suffrage headquarters." Concealing scraps of paper, Lucy had kept a record of their first three days at Occoquan and smuggled it out of the jail through a family member who'd visited one of the inmates.

"Washington November 17—A diary smuggled out of Occoquan jail by one of the suffragists purports to show that the 31 picket prisoners recently sent here are being handled violently by the guards," the article began, followed by quotes from Lucy's diary.

"Wednesday, November 14—Demanded to see Superintendent Whittaker. Request refused. Mrs. Herndon, the matron, said we would have to wait up all night. One of the men guards said he would 'put us in a sardine box and put mustard on us.' Superintendent Whittaker came at 9 p. m. He refused to hear our demand for political rights," she wrote of her first night back at Occoquan. What was her punishment for requesting political rights?

"Seized by guards from behind, flung off my feet, and shot out of the room. All of us were seized by men guards and dragged to cells in men's part. Dorothy Day was roughly used— back twisted. Mrs. Mary A. Nolan (73-year-old picket from Jacksonville, Florida) flung into cell. Mrs. Lawrence Lewis shot past my cell. I slept with Dorothy Day in a single bed," she wrote of the violence that several of the women experienced. She relayed the guards' brutal treatment of her after she asked for an update on the other women's condition.

"I was handcuffed all night and manacled to the bars part of the time for asking the others how they were, and was threatened with a straitjacket and a buckle gag."

Though she didn't know it at the time, the guards at the district jail had threatened Alice Paul in a similar way. Refusing to allow her to see her physician and meet with her attorney, Dudley Malone, they instead sent her to be evaluated for the psychiatric ward. The next day, Lucy confronted the superintendent.

"Thursday, November 16—Asked for Whittaker, who came. He seized Julia Emory by the back of her neck and threw her into the room very brutally. She is a little girl. I asked for counsel to learn the status of the case. I was told to 'shut up,' and was again threatened with a straitjacket and a buckle gag. Later I was taken to put on prison clothes, refused and resisted strenuously. I was then put in a room where delirium tremens patients are kept."

Lucy's creative courage in writing down what was happening on the night of terror—as the night of November 14, 1917, was later called—proved pivotal, especially as the women engaged in a hunger strike. Once the scraps of paper were smuggled out of the prison, they were brought to NWP headquarters. The secretary sent telegrams to the press, as well as to their state-leadership contacts. Their Colorado coordinator sent a telegram of Lucy's diary to President Wilson, his cabinet, and the Washington, D.C., commissioners.

"Thirty suffragists at the work house are being treated with incredible brutality. 60 men are acting as guards. An old lady of 73 years was flung into a cell. A young girl seized by the back of her neck and thrown out of a room. Another girl's back was twisted. Superintendent Whitaker of the work house shook his fist at and threatened Mrs. Lawrence Lewis. Miss Lucy Burns' hands were manacled to the bars of her cell," the *Colorado Springs Gazette* published on November 18 about the night of terror.

The telegram called on President Wilson to end the violence

against the women. "In the name of humanity, will you not act at once to stop the national disgrace of brutal treatment of national women's party in Occoquan and District jail? No civilized country treats political prisoners with such inhumane cruelty."

But when the mother of the youngest imprisoned suffragist appealed to President Wilson's secretary, who was a family friend, he assured her that her daughter was in safe hands and that the stories of inhumane treatment at Occoquan were false.

Another imprisoned suffragist was Mrs. John Winters Brannan, daughter of the founder of the *New York Sun*. She wrote an affidavit about her experience during the night of terror.

"I . . . saw one of the guards seize her [Lucy Burns] by the arms, twist or force them back of her, and one or two other guards seize her by the shoulders, shaking her violently." Fearing that she would also be attacked, the woman put on her heavy sealskin coat. "I was trembling at the time and was stunned with terror at the situation as it had developed."

"I . . . saw the guards seizing the different women of the party with the utmost violence, the furniture being overturned and the room a scene of the utmost disturbance. I saw Miss Lincoln lying on the floor, with every appearance of having just been thrown down by the two guards who were standing over her in a menacing attitude."

"The whole group of women were thrown, dragged or herded out of the office on to the porch, down the steps to the ground, and forced to cross the road . . . to the Administration Building," she wrote, pointing out that Superintendent Whittaker directed the attack and ordered them thrown into different cells in the men's prison.

"There was no privacy for the women, and if any of us wished to undress we would be subject to the view or observation of the guards who remained in the corridor and who could at any moment look at us," she wrote of her experience in the men's section of the prison. "Furthermore, the water closets (toilets) were in full view of the corridor where Superintendent Whittaker and the guards were moving about. The flushing of these closets could only be done from the corridor, and we were forced to ask the guards to do this for us,—the men who had shortly before attacked us," she testified in her affidavit, noting that the guards made terrifying noises by banging the doors and clanging the bars.

When she tried to ask about one of her fellow suffragists, Superintendent Whittaker shouted at her. "Stop that; not another word from your mouth, or I will handcuff you, gag you and put you in a strait jacket." None of the women matrons or employees appeared throughout the night.

"I was exhausted by what I had seen and been through, and spent the night in absolute terror of further attack and of what might still be in store for us. I thought of the young girls who were with us and feared for their safety. The guards . . . acted brutal in the extreme."

Because the charge of obstructing traffic didn't justify the sentences they received, Mrs. Brannan concluded that higher authorities had allowed Whittaker to treat them brutally. "It seemed to me that everything had been done from the time we reached the workhouse to terrorize us, and my fear lest the extreme of outrage would be worked upon the young girls of our party became intense," she wrote. "It is impossible for me to describe the terror of that night."

A week into her six-month sentence and hunger strike, Lucy was moved to the district jail in D.C., where she and Alice were force-fed through their nostrils multiple times. The tactic was vomit-inducing.

The negative publicity from Lucy's published diary saved her life. Her quick thinking to write about their brutal treatment on scraps of paper and smuggle them out of jail was a form of creative courage. The tactic had a positive effect. Two weeks later, the newspapers published the news:

"Twenty-two Woman's Party hunger strikers are released from jail," the *Dallas Morning News* ran as a headline on

November 28, 1917, noting that Lucy Burns and Alice Paul were among them.

"Woman's party headquarters exultantly announced that the jail officials 'had gotten enough' of the first American hunger strike. . . . What higher official ordered this action was not disclosed."

They publicly announced that they would stop their picketing temporarily, in the hopes that President Wilson would mention suffrage in his next address or his State of the Union address to Congress. Their atypical, innovative courage would soon pay off. While many bumps were still ahead, the tide had turned for the federal suffrage amendment.

Did President Wilson call for women's suffrage in his annual message to Congress in December 1917? No, but he did send a signal.

"Wilson comes out for suffrage amendment," was the *Pueblo Chieftan's* headline on January 10, 1918, the day that the House of Representatives voted on the Susan B. Anthony federal suffrage amendment.

Calling on the president the day before, twelve Democratic House members sought Wilson's view on how he wanted them to vote on the federal suffrage amendment. A large majority of House Republicans planned to support it.

"The committee found that the president had not felt at liberty to volunteer his advice to members of Congress in this important matter but when we sought his advice, he very frankly and earnestly advised us to vote for the amendment as an act of right and justice to the women of the country and of the world."

Headlines across the nation broadcasted the outcome, including Chicago's *Broad Ax*, which had often run articles about or by Ida May Wells. "The Susan B. Anthony amendment to the federal Constitution was approved by the House of

Representatives by a 2/3 majority vote, vote being 274 to 136," the *Broad Ax* relayed, noting that every member from Illinois voted for it.

The coincidence of the date was not lost on members of the NWP, who celebrated with a dinner at a Washington, D.C., establishment. The House had voted on January 10, 1918, exactly a year after the women had begun their pickets. Though it was the first positive vote in the House since Susan B. Anthony first called on Congress to pass it, it wouldn't be the last.

"The amendment now goes to the Senate and if that body passes it, the woman's next fight will be before the state legislatures for adoption."

Other good news came for the picketers in March, when a judge declared the arrests of the 218 suffragists to be illegal. He expunged their records. Though many picketed again when the Senate failed to have taken a vote by August 1918, they were given short sentences in a better jail. With the Democrat-controlled Senate two votes shy of passing the amendment, President Wilson took a bold and unusual move.

"I regard the concurrence of the Senate in the constitutional amendment proposing the extension of the suffrage to women as vital and essential to the successful prosecution of the Great War of Humanity in which we are engaged," President Wilson said in a speech he gave to the Senate in support of the amendment on September 30, 1918.

"Are we alone to ask and take the utmost that women can give—service and sacrifice of every kind—and still say that we do not see what title that gives them to stand by our sides in the guidance of the affairs of their nation and ours? We have made partners of the women in this war; shall we admit them only to a partnership of sacrifice and suffering and toil and not to be a partnership of privilege and of right?"

When the Senate voted the next day, the amendment was still two votes shy. "His speech, eloquent as it was, could not break down the opposition in the Senate which he had so long protected and condoned," NWP leader Doris Stevens reflected, noting that the president could have campaigned for pro-suffrage senators when recent vacancies occurred.

The NWP kept the pressure on, again calling on women voters in the West, and now New York, to hold the party in power accountable in the 1918 midterms. This time, Republicans were elected to take over the U.S. House and Senate. Not only that, but World War I also ended with the collapse of Germany and an armistice on November 11, 1918.

On New Year's Day 1919, the Silent Sentinels burned the president's speeches in an urn called a watch fire and held ceremonies at Lafayette Square. Less than a month later, President Wilson included women's suffrage for the first time in his annual address to the Congress. "What should we say of the women—of their intelligence, quickening every task that they touched; their capacity for organization and cooperation, which gave their action discipline and enhanced the effectiveness of everything they attempted . . . the least tribute we can pay them is to make them the equals of men and political rights, as they have proved themselves their equals in every field of practical work they have entered, whether for themselves or their country."

But Wilson's eloquence wasn't enough. Despite the sentinels holding watch fires, only one senator changed his vote, leaving the Susan B. Anthony amendment one vote shy of passing the Senate when the Sixty-Fifth Congress concluded on March 4, 1919.

The first session of the new Sixty-Sixth Congress wasn't scheduled to being until December 1919, months away. Not wanting to wait, the new Republican Congress called a special session on May 19, 1919. Two days later, on May 21, the House of Representatives passed the Susan B. Anthony amendment, the Nineteenth Amendment to the Constitution, by a vote of 304 to 89. This was forty-two votes more than the necessary two-thirds majority. Within two weeks, the Senate voted, too.

"Women Win in Senate; Fight Goes to States," was the

headline in the *Jackson City Patriot* of Jackson, Michigan. Some newspapers ran pictures of suffrage leaders, including Carrie Chapman Catt, Dr. Anna Howard Shaw, Alice Paul, and Lucy Burns. (Today, the Lucy Burns Museum memorializes the story of women's suffrage and her prison experience at the Workhouse Arts Center, the site of the former prison, in Lorton, Virginia.)

The U.S. Senate passed the Nineteenth Amendment to the Constitution by a margin of sixty-six to thirty on June 4, 1919. Of the forty-nine Republicans in the Senate, forty voted for it and nine voted against it. Of the forty-seven Democrats, twenty-six voted for it with twenty-one against. "Amendment wins after 40 years of struggle," the *Oregonian* and others reported. "Suffrage Now Up to States," the *Baltimore Sun* reported of the final phase.

11
REMEMBERING A LADY

Why did women's suffrage drive a state legislator to the ledge of the state capitol building? Was it politics? Public sentiment? The love of a lady? The fight for ratification took a surprising, unpredictable turn in August 1920. Did he take the plunge?

As soon as the U.S. Senate passed the Susan B. Anthony amendment in June 1919, granting women the right to vote, the ratification process by state legislatures began. Carrie Chapman Catt called on the network NAWSA had created to press the states to call special sessions to pass the amendment. Of the forty-eight state legislatures, thirty-six needed to pass the measure to complete ratification and make the Nineteenth Amendment part of the U.S. Constitution. The clock was ticking to pass it so that women in all states could vote in the 1920 presidential election in November.

By August 1920, thirty-fives states had voted for the amendment, but several southern states had rejected it. Of the few states left to vote, Tennessee seemed to have the best odds, but victory was not guaranteed. Worse, Tennessee's Governor Albert Roberts had refused to call a special session of the Tennessee General Assembly, despite pressure from President Woodrow Wilson. Politics had given Roberts reason to pause.

Because he had supported a tax increase, he was unsure whether he would win the August 5 primary race for reelection. But he did. After this, Governor Roberts called a special session in August for the Tennessee General Assembly to take up ratifying the Nineteenth Amendment. Victory for national suffrage now hinged on Tennessee.

Suffragists and anti-suffragist organizations poured into Nashville, Tennessee, and packed the lobbies of the city's hotels to talk to as many legislators as they could. The suffragists knew that Tennessee was their best hope but feared a close vote. Unlike some issues, suffrage crossed party lines. The question was: Were there enough votes to make Tennessee the thirty-sixth and winning state for suffrage? What would it come down to?

One legislator in particular, who felt tremendous pressure from the lobbying and the vice grip of politics, was Harry Burn, a rare Republican in a mostly Democratic state from the town of Niota in McMinn County in East Tennessee. Though he was in only his first term in the General Assembly, Harry had received phone calls from prominent politicians after he arrived in Nashville for the special session. Both the Republican presidential candidate Warren G. Harding and Democratic presidential candidate James Cox called him.

"They were both supporting ratification,"[11] Harry said, noting that he also received a telegram from the chairman of the Republican National Committee asking him to vote for suffrage. But the telegrams that the made strongest impression on him were those he received from his constituents. At this point in his very young political career, their voices mattered more to him than the national Republican leadership.

"Strong opposition here to suffrage amendment we want it defeated," one telegram from his hometown declared. Another

---

[11] *Tyler Boyd Tennessee Statesman Harry T. Burn.* See page 203 for this chapter's endnotes.

sent a concerning message: "Ninety percent of your friends and the people of McMinn County are expecting you to vote against ratification and not to violate your oath of office." Still others were downright threatening: "A vote for it will defeat you in spite of hell."

Reelection was very much on Harry's mind. He'd only been elected once. Legislators are most vulnerable to defeat in their first reelection effort. If only 10 percent of his district supported suffrage, as the telegrams suggested, why should he vote for it? Would he lose his seat if he did?

Yet he knew the telegrams and phone calls, along with handshakes of the suffragists and anti-suffragists filling the lobbies of the hotels, were designed "to agitate, one way or the other, or persuade."

Not only was Harry a first-termer, but he was also the youngest member of Tennessee's General Assembly. How did a twenty-three-year-old banker get elected to the state legislature? He had a political backer, and a big one, in Herschel Candler, the Tennessee state senator from Harry's hometown. A sixteen-year veteran in the Tennessee Senate, Herschel had once served as a mayor, which had given him significant political power in McMinn County.

In the Tennessee Senate in the special session, Herschel had given a bitter speech against suffrage. In fact, he was the most anti-suffrage member of the senate. The reason? There were many, but one stood out. A year earlier, Herschel had lost an election for mayor of Athens. Why? A new law had given women limited suffrage, allowing them to vote in a local election. Herschel had lost his bid for Athens mayor by twenty-seven votes. The woman's vote had gone against him: Forty-nine women in McMinn County voted against his election.

"I don't like the class of women here lobbying for this bill," Herschel had said in his anti-suffrage speech, noting that these women weren't mothers. Though the lobbies of the hotels in Nashville were full of women asking legislators for the vote, the Hermitage hotel was ground zero for their efforts.

Herschel attacked NAWSA president Carrie Chapman Catt in particular. He didn't like being dictated to by "an old woman down here at the Hermitage Hotel, whose name is Catt. . . . I think her husband's name is Tom . . . Mrs. Catt is nothing more than an anarchist."

Catt's husband George had died years earlier, which made Herschel's comment even more insensitive. "If there is anything I despise, it is a man who is under petticoat government."

Herschel's "petticoat speech" put a lot of pressure on Harry to vote against suffrage. What would happen in the upcoming election if he bucked his mentor? Surely he would lose reelection without Herschel's support.

Even worse, Harry was staying next door to Herschel at their hotel. He couldn't get away from him. To avoid taking up residence at the Hermitage hotel, the McMinn County legislators had booked a row of rooms at Hotel Tulane for the special session. Harry's single room was adjacent to the two rooms occupied by Herschel. Herschel's position hung over him. He also couldn't escape the roses in the lobby. Which color did he have the courage to wear? Yellow or red? Holding particular meaning in the context of the final vote, both were creative signs of courage.

Harry T. Burn,
1918 (T. Boyd,
Wikimedia Commons)

★ ★ ★ ★ ★

Harry observed that Catt and the suffragists were "beautifully organized." Yellow roses on a legislator's lapel indicated a "yes" vote for the Nineteenth Amendment. Red roses signaled a "no" vote. Both NAWSA and NWP had sent delegations to use logic and reason to persuade lawmakers. Becoming indignant and frustrated, both suffrage groups discovered that the anti-suffragists were using any means they could to convince Tennessee's legislators to vote against the amendment. One suffragist leader explained that some legislators backed out of their pledges to them after they were "baited with whiskey, tempted with money and every other device."

Both sides were also keeping a tally prior to the vote of the commitments they had received. NWP's Anita Pollitzer had met with Harry. When she asked him for his support, he gave an evasive reply. "I cannot pledge myself, but I will do nothing to hurt you," Harry cryptically conveyed. What did he mean?

Anita was so worried about his lack of commitment that she immediately called the Republican Party chairman for McMinn County. The next day, Harry received a letter from another prominent Tennessee politician telling him he wouldn't have a future in politics if he didn't vote for suffrage. Harry, however, was worried that if he voted for suffrage, he would lose his next election. "The majority of my constituency demands that I vote against ratification." The question was: What did Harry believe was just and right? Would he prove a statesman or a politician?

As the session opened, the political pressure from the lobbying, politicians, and telegrams was getting to Harry so much that he couldn't sleep. Checking out of his hotel, he stayed at a friend's house. "I tell you, the only way that you got any rest . . . was to not let them know where you were."

The chatter in the newspapers made Harry's tension even worse. The day before the vote, headlines from around the nation reported that the outcome was too close to call. "Vote on suffrage to be close, say 'Pro's and 'Antis'," the *Times-Picayune* of New Orleans published. "Tennessee leaders on both sides claim victory on eve of the battle."

Though the Tennessee Senate had passed the measure, the outcome in the Tennessee House was calculated at a tie. One pivotal politician was certain that he knew the outcome, as the press relayed. "Seth Walker, speaker and leader of the opposition, said the amendment would be rejected. 'We have ratification beaten, that is all there is to it,' he declared."

★ ★ ★ ★ ★

Though the political pressure was strong, at least the yellow and red roses on the lapels of lawmakers gave off a pleasant aroma as the lawmakers arrived at the capitol the morning of August 18, 1920. In mid morning, Harry received another letter, hand-delivered by a page. This one was particularly meaningful. Soon it was time to attend the session.

"As he walked onto the House floor, Burn had pinned to his jacket lapel a red rose representing his intent to vote against suffrage."

When an NWP member saw his red rose, she spoke out with disappointment, "We really trusted you, Mr. Burn."

Despite the red rose, the truth was that no one knew what he was going to do, not even his mother. His pledge not to hurt the NWP members contradicted the red rose. "The gallery of the Capitol was packed as it has never been since," Harry recalled. "Nothing as big or intense ever happened again in the Tennessee legislature."

During the session, Harry twice voted against the amendment but only on procedural grounds that delayed the final vote. When the speaker saw that the procedural votes were virtually tied at forty-eight, he seized the opportunity to kill suffrage in Tennessee by calling for a final vote on the actual amendment.

"Believing the amendment would fail on a vote for the resolution itself, Speaker Walker called for a vote on the 'merits' of the resolution."

Harry knew this was it. This was the time to act on the pledge he had made to himself. He'd played the part of a politician by voting to delay the vote, but if it came down to voting on the merits of the bill, and if his vote was needed to win, he knew what he needed to do.

"The roll call began. Anderson and Bell voted aye. Bond, Boyd, Boyer and Bratton voted no. Next on the list was Harry T. Burn, sitting on the third row to the right of the rostrum."

The suffragists and anti-suffragists in the gallery followed along with their alphabetical lists of pre-pledged votes. When Harry's name was called, what did he do?

"'Aye,' Harry said quickly. Some didn't even hear his vote. He had answered in such haste that some thought he might have mistakenly voted to ratify. He then removed the red rose from the lapel of his jacket," a family member recalled of Harry's courage to change his mind.

While the speaker expected a forty-eight to forty-eight vote like the procedural votes, the final roll call was forty-nine to forty-seven. In order to make sure the vote wasn't in dispute, the speaker changed his vote to "yes," making the final tally fifty to forty-six. Of the ninety-six members in attendance, Democrats voted for suffrage by a vote of thirty-five to thirty-four, and Republicans voted for it by a vote of fifteen to twelve. What happened immediately after the vote?

"It was pandemonium. There is no better word to describe the House chamber after the vote. Like a room full of graduates tossing their caps into the air upon commencement, the suffragists in the gallery tossed their yellow roses into the air. They screamed, sang and danced in joy. The noises of celebration carried all the way down the hill at the Hermitage."

What happened to Harry right after the vote?

Under the shower of yellow roses on the General Assembly's floor, Harry was thrust into the crosshairs of activity. The chief sergeant at arms immediately approached Harry to let him know of threats made against him because of his vote. The governor had ordered him to send his crew of men to protect Harry. He wanted to keep him on the house floor until state troopers could arrive to shield him from the mob.

Thinking this was silly, Harry resisted having two or three young men working for the sergeant at arms hover around him. But he also wanted to avoid the mob. After waiting with them for a few minutes, he slipped away to an office on the House floor facing the speaker's office. He also made a phone call. "I just stepped inside the door and slammed it and locked it. When I went in there I went over and looked out the window and there was a ledge," Harry recalled.

Calculating that his slender frame could navigate fifteen feet on a ledge, Harry sought to get away from the guards of the sergeant at arms. Did he jump? Hardly. "So, I just walked that ledge down to the portico and then went on across and went in what was then the state library."

When the young guards saw him, they ran after him, like dogs hunting a fox. "But I outran them. I ran to the Hermitage Hotel. It must have been six or eight hundred feet." When he arrived at the Hermitage hotel, he pulled out a pair of glasses and changed the angle of his hat so he could mingle undetected. After catching up with a friend, he left and drove around the rest of the day to avoid the mob seeking the man whose changed vote had given women the right to vote.

One crucial person, however, found him before midnight. A reporter with the *Nashville Tennessean* had a tip that a rival newspaper was publishing an article the next morning accusing Harry of accepting a bribe to change his vote.

"No human being has made any propositions to me," Harry said in a statement published in the *Tennessean* the next day.

His name soon filled the newspapers around the nation. "Youngest member of legislature said he cast ballot for suffrage without being unduly influenced," the *Seattle Daily Times* proclaimed.

How did Harry's backer, Herschel Candler, respond to both Harry's vote and the accusations of bribery against him afterwards? The *Chattanooga News* had gotten the scoop. "Terrible pressure was put on me to influence Burn's vote. I refused. He has the same right to his conscience that I have. I have never asked him to vote one way or the other on suffrage," Herschel said, explaining that he didn't know in advance which way Harry was going to vote. He also defended Harry against the bribery accusations.

"Harry, I've known you all my life. I know you go to your convictions. I honor you for it. Don't let these dirty scandals shake you." Knowing him from childhood, Herschel added, "You can't make a crook overnight." He didn't believe the rumors one bit.

Harry suspected the root of the false news about him taking a bribe came from the conversation he'd had with fellow legislator Joe Hanover after the vote. Hanover had come up to him, put his arm on his shoulder and said, "Harry, that was the most valuable vote you have ever cast. In a man's lifetime that will be worth more to you than anything you have ever done." Someone overheard the phrase "valuable vote" and misinterpreted its meaning as a bribe. A big supporter of suffrage, Hanover saw the long-term significance of Harry's vote.

The press didn't have the real scoop, at least not yet.

The next morning, August 19, Harry sent a statement to the house clerk, who read it on the floor. "I desire to resent in the name of honesty and justice the veiled intimation and accusation regarding my vote on the suffrage amendment as indicated by certain statements," his response began. Then he refuted the bribery charges. "And it is my sincere belief that those responsible for their existence know there is not a scintilla of truth in them," he wrote.

"I know they are false, and I feel that my association amongst you has enabled you to know me well enough that you unanimously join me in resenting the same."

He explained why he changed his vote to favor ratification. "First, I believe in full suffrage as a right. Second, I believe we had a moral and legal right to ratify," Harry explained of the justice behind his vote. What he said next stood out as a surprise.

"Third, I know that a mother's advice is always safest for her boy to follow, and my mother wanted me to vote for ratification," he said, reflecting on the letter he'd received from her the morning of the vote.

"Fourth, I appreciated the fact that an opportunity such as seldom comes to moral man—to free American women from political slavery—was mine. Fifth, I desire that my party, and both state and nation, might say that it was a Republican from the mountains of Tennessee."

The next morning, the news about his mother's influence spread like wildfire in the press. "Followed his mother's advice. Why Tennessean voted yes," the *Seattle Daily Times* published. "Mother proud of son who cast deciding vote for suffrage," the *New York Daily Tribune* reported August 21. Finding Harry's mother, Febb Burn, at her farm in McMinn County, the *New York Daily Tribune* and others had asked her to weigh in.

"I am glad he loved me enough to say afterward that my letter had so much influence on him," his mother proudly said. "The first news I heard of the suffrage victory was from Harry himself. He called me over the long-distance telephone immediately after the Wednesday session to tell me the suffrage amendment had carried and that it had been his vote which assured the victory."

What had motivated Febb to write Harry and ask for him to vote for suffrage? Angry about Herschel Candler's anti-suffrage speech and cognizant of his influence on her son, Febb Burn picked up a pencil and wrote Harry a letter.

"Hurrah, and vote for suffrage and don't keep them in doubt. I noticed Candler's speech, it was very bitter," Febb wrote on the fourth page. Though she and Harry had talked about the issue, she wasn't sure where he stood. She knew he was worried about reelection.

"But I do hope you are still in the notion of not making the race this fall. I hope you see enough of politicians to know it is not one of the greatest things to be one. What say you?" she asked.

Referring to Herschel Candler's "tomcat" slam of Carrie Chapman Catt, she turned the slam into a play on words for suffrage. "Don't forget to be a good boy and help Mrs. 'Thomas Catt' with her 'rats.' Is she the one that put rat in ratification? Ha! No more from Mama this time. With lots of love, Mama."

Harry had done what Abigail Adams had wanted her husband to do in 1776. This unmarried man remembered the ladies by remembering the most important lady to him: his mother.

"In regard to suffrage, my mother caused me to take the view I did. I have always been for suffrage as a matter of moral right, but had planned to vote against, thinking that I would represent a majority of my constituents until I received this letter. I voted for it, casting the deciding vote, and I expect to stand by it," he said in his response on the statehouse floor.

In some ways, the notion of suffrage began with Abigail's decision to take initiative with her husband by asking him to remember the ladies in March 1776. It was fitting that a family relationship had made a difference in the final vote that gave women around the nation the right to vote.

Harry had heard his mother talk about the justice of giving women the vote, as she relayed to newspapers. "I believe it is just a matter of rights. I have taken very little interest in the campaign and don't know the principal suffrage leaders," Febb told the *New York Daily Tribune.* "But I did know that the contest was on in the Tennessee legislature and I just kept hoping and praying that Harry would vote *aye.* I thought all the time that he would vote for it, although he had never told me definitively just how he intended to vote."

When the nation was founded, states gave voting rights to men who owned land. Perhaps it was fitting, too, that Febb

Burn was a landowner and widow who ran a farm. The workers on her farm had the right to vote but she did not. Just as Elizabeth Cady Stanton had gained a vision for the vote years earlier after seeing the injustice done to widows who lost their land, so Febb saw this as an injustice to correct.

"I have hired hands on my farm right here who pay no taxes, yet they are permitted to vote. But I do pay taxes and have not had any hand in my country's affairs," Febb said.

Like Inez Milholland years earlier, who hoped that women's suffrage would stamp out corruption in politics, so Febb hoped that women would have a positive effect on the process. "I think suffrage will purify politics and I am for progress."

Harry implemented a form of creative courage, the courage to change his mind and do what was right and just.

Carrie Chapman Catt concluded that suffrage had been a quest of perseverance, a quality that Sojourner Truth had demonstrated. Likewise, the ratification effort had required resilience. Like Ida Wells-Barnett, Catt's NAWSA and Lucy Burns's NWP had to bounce back, and they made a final push in the lobby of the Tennessee statehouse. Perhaps the biggest obstacle to suffrage was politics. Too many legislators had prioritized politics over justice.

"Had more statesmen and fewer politicians directed the policies of parties, women would have been enfranchised in the years between 1865 and 1880 and American history, along many lines, would have changed its course," Carrie Chapman Catt, president of the National American Woman Suffrage Association, reflected on the role that politics played in delaying women winning the vote in all states. She blamed "the deflecting and the thwarting of public sentiment, through the trading and the trickery, the buying and the selling of American politics." The ratification process was no different.

"But when the final victory came, women were alternately indignant that it had been so long in coming, and amazed that it had come at all."

Harry Burn's great-grandnephew wrote a book about him and fittingly called it *Tennessee Statesman Harry Burn: Woman Suffrage, Free Elections and a Life of Service.* Harry T. Burn won his reelection in 1920 and spent 55 years in public service. He showed the value of justice and the courage to change his mind, a valuable quality that is relevant today. He chose statesmanship over politics.

ENDNOTES

Chapter 1: Initiating Independence

Page #

3 "On such a" Abigail Adams to John Adams, March 2, 1776.

4 "But I never" John Adams to Abigail Adams, Dec. 3, 1775.

4 "I wish I" John Adams to Abigail Adams, Feb. 16, 1776.

4 "I pray my dear" Ibid.

4 "I think you" John Adams to Abigail Adams, May 27, 1776.

5 "Nothing has" John Adams to Abigail Adams, May 22, 1776.

5 "This has been" Ibid.

5 "Is there no" John Adams to Abigail Adams, April 28, 1776.

5 "I suppose" Abigail Adams to John Adams, Dec. 10, 1775.

6 "One is that" Ibid.

6 "I cannot conclude" Ibid.

6 "They raise" Ibid.

7 "I have been" Abigail Adams to John Adams, March 2, 1776.

7 "But hark!" Ibid.

7 "I have been" Ibid.

7 "Your distresses" John Adams to Abigail Adams, March 19, 1776.

7 "I am charmed" Abigail Adams to John Adams, March 2, 1776.

7 "'Tis highly prized" Ibid.

7 "I have spread" Abigail Adams to John Adams, Feb. 21, 1776.

8 "Perhaps the" Thomas Paine, *Common Sense*, 1776, digital ed.

8 "It has been" John Adams to Abigail Adams, March 19, 1776.

8 "absolute power" Thomas Paine, *Common Sense*, 1776, digital ed.

8 "There is something" Ibid.

8 "The state of" Ibid.

9 "The prejudice" Ibid.

9 "But there is" Ibid.

9 "Their form" Ibid.

9 "requested a king" Ibid.

9 "Which is the" Ibid.

9 "that it is the" Ibid.

9 "Even the distance" Ibid.

9 "Everything that" Ibid.

10 "I want to know" Abigail Adams to John Adams, March 2, 1776.

10 "I dare say" Ibid.

10 "On such a" Ibid.

10 "You ask, what" John Adams to Abigail Adams, March 19, 1776.

10 "But all agree" Ibid.

11 "This writer seems" Ibid.

11 "I feel very" Abigail Adams to John Adams, March 31, 1776.

11 "We knew not" Ibid.
11 "I long to hear" Ibid.
11 "I have this" John Adams to Abigail Adams, May 17, 1776.
12 "He concluded" Ibid.
12 "Is it not" Ibid.
12 "Great Britain" Ibid.
12 "Yesterday the" John Adams to Abigail Adams, July 3, 1776.
12 "You will see" Ibid.
13 "Time has been" Ibid.
13 "This will cement" Ibid.
13 "We hold these" *Declaration of Independence*, July 4, 1776.
14 "Man being" John Locke, *Two Treatises of Government*, 1689, digital ed.
14 "Hath by nature" Ibid.
14 "law of nature" Ibid.
14 "is limited" Ibid.
14 "have a right" Ibid.

Chapter 2: Remembering the Ladies
Page #
18 "I need not" Abigail Adams to Edward Dilly, May 22, 1775.
18 "The spirit that" Ibid.
19 "And by the" Abigail Adams to John Adams, March 31, 1776.
19 "Do not put" Ibid.
19 "If particular care" Ibid.
19 "That your sex are" Ibid.
19 "Why then" Ibid.
21 "Regard us then" Ibid.
20 "Laws and government" Ibid.
21 "In order to" Ibid.
20 "Whatever" John Locke, *Two Treatises of Government*, 1689, digital ed.
22 "Every member" Ibid.
20 "for it was" Ibid.
22 "And yet a" Ibid.
20 "Must not she" Ibid.
22 "But yet by fiction" Ibid.
20 "If it be said" Ibid.
20 "As to your" John Adams to Abigail Adams, April 14, 1776.
23 "The scars" Ibid.
20 "But your letter" Ibid.
24 "For where" Ibid.
21 "Depend upon it" Ibid.
24 "Thus, Sir, the" Ibid.
24 "But in the" Ibid.

21 "We dare not" Ibid.
21 "A new assembly" James Sullivan to Elbridge Gerry, May 17, 1776.
25 "It is certain" John Adams to James Sullivan, May 26, 1776.
25 "But let us" Ibid.
25 "But why exclude" Ibid.
25 "Is it not equally" Ibid.
25 "If this is" Ibid.
25 "Such is the frailty" Ibid.
26 "Your idea" Ibid.
26 "The same reasoning" Ibid.
26 "For generally speaking" Ibid.
26 "There will be" Ibid.
26 "If the multitude" Ibid.
27 "The times" U.S. Constitution, 1787.
27 "Nay I believe" John Adams to James Sullivan, May 26, 1776.
27 "The only possible" Ibid.
28 "The Christian" Thomas Jefferson, Draft *Declaration of Independence*, 1776
29 "But what do" John Adams to Hezekiah Niles, Feb. 13, 1818.
29 "The revolution" Ibid.
29 "This radical change" Ibid.
29 "The colonies had" Ibid.
29 "By what means" Ibid.
30 "I wish you" Elizabeth Shaw to Abigail Adams, Dec. 29, 1793.
30 "took the" Elizabeth Stanton, *Eighty Years and More*, 1898, 3.
30 "took the responsibility" Ibid.
30 "On General Washington's" Ibid.
31 "admitted that" Ibid., 3-4.

Chapter 3: Vision for the Vote
Page #
32 "Fairly at sea" Elizabeth Stanton, *Eighty Years*, 1898, 73.
33 "Mr. Birney" Ibid.
33 "I soon perceived" Ibid.
33 "I was always" Ibid.
34 "Well what" Ibid., 74.
34 "I heard you" Ibid.
34 "You went to" Ibid.
34 "Bless me" Ibid.
34 "I should have" Ibid.
35 "I commenced" Ibid., 2.
35 "My only brother" Ibid., 20.
35 "We early felt" Ibid.
35 "Well do I" Ibid.

35 "Oh, my daughter" Ibid.
35 "I will try" Ibid., 21.
35 "I thought that" Ibid.
36 "I taxed" Ibid., 22.
36 "Ah, you should" Ibid., 23.
36 "In our Scotch" Ibid., 31.
36 "Hence it made" Ibid.
36 "The tears and" Ibid.
36 "As the practice" Ibid.
36 "The students" Ibid., 32.
37 "One Christmas" Ibid.
37 "Now if" Ibid.
37 "But my mind" Ibid., 33-4.
37 "With this constant" Ibid., 32.
37 "Becoming more" Ibid., 31.
37 "When you are grown" Ibid.
38 "Though I was" Ibid., 33.
38 "When those" Ibid.
38 "Again I felt" Ibid., 33-4.
38 "Mr. Stanton was" Ibid., 59.
38 "As I had" Ibid., 58.
38 "I had become" Ibid., 60.
39 "the most eloquent" Ibid., 58.
39 "I shall never" Ibid., 59.
39 "It seemed to" Ibid.
39 "I felt a new inspiration" Ibid.
39 "Is it good" Ibid, 75.
40 "He felt the rebuke" Ibid.
40 "I think the" *The Liberator*, June 12, 1840.
40 "If Victoria can" Ibid.
41 "It struck me" Ibid., 75.
40 "My husband made" Elizabeth Stanton, *Eighty Years*, 1898, 79.
41 "Though women" Ibid.
41 "Judging from" Ibid., 80.
41 "After battling" Ibid., 81.
41 "Having strongly" Ibid., 82.
42 "She had not" Ibid., 81.
42 "Male and female" Lucretia Mott, *Discourse on Women*, 1850, 4.
42 "He gave" Ibid.
42 "The acquaintance" Elizabeth Stanton, *Eighty Years*, 1898, 82.
42 "It was intensely" Ibid.
43 "As Mrs. Mott" Ibid., 81-2.
43 "As the convention" Ibid., 81.

43 "The action of this" Ibid.

43 "Then, too, the" Ibid., 144.

43 "Up to this" Ibid., 147.

43 "The house" Ibid., 144.

43 "My father gave" Ibid.

44 "I urged him" Ibid.

44 "my duties were" Ibid., 147.

44 "My experience" Ibid., 148.

45 "The general discontent" Ibid., 147-8.

45 "A healthy discontent" Ibid., 147.

45 "I could not see" Ibid., 148.

45 "There I met" Ibid.

45 "My discontent" Ibid.

46 "The convention" Ibid.

46 Ibid.

46 "When, in the" *The Liberator*, Aug. 24, 1848.

47 "We hold these" Ibid.

47 "The history" Ibid.

47 "to demand" Ibid.

47 "usurpations on" Ibid.

47 "Has never" Ibid.

47 "in the formation" Ibid.

47 "ignorant and" Ibid.

48 "Having deprived" Ibid.

48 "He has made" Ibid.

48 "He has monopollized" Ibid.

48 "He has denied" Ibid.

48 "He has created" Ibid.

48 "He has usurped" Ibid.

49 l the journals" Ibid.

50 "Our friends gave" Ibid.

50 "The same year" Ibid.

50 "Hence the demands" Ibid.

51 "The effect of" Ibid.

51 "I think all women" Ibid.

49 "Now in view" Ibid.

49 "Hear, O man" *The Vermont Mercury*, Aug. 4, 1848, 2.

49 "The women in" *Westchester Herald*, Aug. 8, 1848.

49 "It is evident" Ibid.

49 "It seems" *Semiweekly Eagle*, Aug. 17, 1848.

50 "No words could" Elizabeth Stanton, *Eighty Years*, 1898, 149.

50 "With our Declaration" Ibid.

50 "All the journals"

50 "Our friends gave" Ibid.
50 "The same year" Ibid.
50 "Hence the demands" Ibid.
51 "The effect of" Ibid.
51 "I think all women" Ibid.

Chapter 4: Persevering Truth & Faith
Page #
54 "A large old-fashioned" Sojourner Truth, *Narrative*, 1852, 9.
54 "This event was noticed" Ibid.
55 "Separated forever" Ibid., 11.
55 "Mau-mau, what" Ibid., 11.
55 "Now the war began" Ibid., 22.
57 "My children there is" Ibid., 11.
57 "A God, Mau-mau!" Ibid., 11.
57 "He lives in the sky" Ibid.
58 "Oh Lord, how long" Ibid.
58 "Those are the same" Ibid.
58 "God, I'm afraid" Ibid., 39.
59 "Yes, that's a good" Ibid., 39.
60 "Why, Bell, so" Ibid., 40.
60 "No, I did not" Ibid.
60 "You must go" Ibid.
60 "No, I did not" Ibid.
60 "Well, I shall" Ibid.
61 "There is but one" Ibid., 41.
61 "Dear me" Ibid., 43.
62 "I'll have my child" Ibid., 42.
62 "Have your child" Ibid.
62 "How can you get him" Ibid.
62 "No, I have no money" Ibid., 42.
62 "I was sure God" Ibid., 42.
63 "Fowler's horse hoveld" Ibid., 50.
63 "That was done" Ibid.
63 "Yes, I swear" Ibid., 46.
63 "sentence of the court" Ibid., 51.
63 "Well, you do look like" Ibid., 52.
63 "Oh, Jesus, look" Ibid.
64 "May I" "Ar'nt I a Woman?" *Anti-Slavery Bugle*, (OH) June 21, 1851.
64 "I have as" Ibid.
64 "I have heard" Ibid.
64 "As for intellect" Ibid.
65 "You need not" Ibid.

65 "Why children" Ibid.

65 "I can't read" Ibid.

65 "The lady has" Ibid.

65 "Man, where is" Ibid.

67 "I am pleased" Ibid.

67 "This is Sojourner" "Abraham Lincoln and Sojourner Truth," *New York Times*, Oct. 29, 2010.

67 "Mr. President, when" Ibid.

67 "I appreciate you" Ibid.

67 "I expect you have" Ibid.

67 "They were all" Ibid.

67 "I thank God that" Ibid.

67 "If the people over" Ibid.

68 "This is beautiful indeed" Ibid.

68 "For Aunty" Ibid.

68 "I felt that I was" Ibid.

Chapter 5: Calculating Strategies
Page #

72 "Her experience" *Daily Illinois State Register*, March 30, 1884.

72 "After 15 years" Ibid.

72 "This contrast" Ibid.

73 "Although a" Carrie Catt, *Woman Suffrage & Politics*, 1923, digital ed.

73 "Where do you" *New York Herald*, May 11, 1861.

73 "At length" Carrie Catt, *Woman Suffrage*, 1923, digital ed.

74 "I wish, Sir" Ibid.

74 "Do you not" Ibid.

74 "The next morning's" Ibid.

74 "Whatever the schoolmasters" Ibid.

74 "The annual national" *Evening Post*, Oct. 19, 1854.

74 "And attracted" *Evening Post*, Oct. 21, 1854.

75 "Miss Stone" Ibid.

75 "Mrs. Susan B. Anthony" Ibid.

75 "She labored" Elizabeth Stanton, *Eighty Years*, 1898, 168.

76 "From 1852" *Daily Illinois State Register*, March 30, 1884.

76 "That so long" *Evening Post,* Oct. 21, 1854.

76 "Resolved that" Ibid.

76 "forged the thunderbolts" Elizabeth Stanton, *Eighty Years*, 1898, 165.

76 "fired them" Ibid., 168.

77 "Governments derive" National Parks Service https://www.nps.gov/wori/learn/historyculture/more-womens-rights-conventions.htm

77 "The political" Ibid.

78 "I offer a petitions" Carrie Catt, *Woman Suffrage*, 1923, digital ed.

78 "But when the" *Our Documents*, www.ourdocuments.gov.

79 "When Congress" Carrie Catt, *Woman Suffrage*, 1923, digital ed.

79 "the ballot for" *New York Herald*, May 11, 1866.

79 "Men and parties" Carrie Catt, *Woman Suffrage*, 1923, digital ed

80 "Your joint resolutions" Ibid.

80 "But the only tenable" Ibid.

80 "With you we" Ibid.

80 "Our demand must" Ibid.

80 "I am not a farmer" Ibid.

81 "Don't wait until" Ibid.

81 "I propose that you" Ibid.

81 "We believe" Ida Harper, *Life & Work Susan B. Anthony*, 1899, 277.

81 "Neither color nor sex" Ibid.

81 "Women and colored" Ibid.

81 "We respectfully" Ibid.

82 "Resolved that as" *New York Herald*, July 5, 1867.

82 "There were but two" *Evening Post*, May 15, 1868.

82 "In the evening a" Ibid.

82 "Republican Party" Ibid.

83 "The discussion did" Ibid.

83 "untimely and" Carrie Catt, *Woman Suffrage*, 1923, digital ed.

83 "All the old friends" Ibid.

83 "engaged in bitterly" Ibid.

83 "George Francis Train" Ibid.

83 "Men, their rights" Ibid.

83 "Since the two men" Ibid.

83 "Because we make" Ibid.

84 "One idea for" Ibid.

85 "Once Mrs. Stanton" Ibid.

85 "With a cynical smile" Ibid.

85 "Impartial suffrage" Ibid.

85 "The moral courage" Ibid.

88 "Susan B. Anthony in trouble" *NY Herald*, Nov. 16, 1872.

88 "having voted" Carrie Catt, *Woman Suffrage*, 1923, digital ed.

89 "There was nothing" *Public Ledger*, Dec. 27, 1872.

89 "Poor Susan B. Anthony" *Pomeroy's Democrat*, Jan. 25, 1873.

89 "This is an outrage" Ibid.

89 "by state" Carrie Catt, *Woman Suffrage*, 1923, digital ed.

89 "The vaults in yonder" Ibid.

90 "Miss Anthony held" Ibid.

90 "Miss Anthony believed" Ibid.

90 "If by the laws" Ibid.

90 "All persons" *Our Documents*, www.ourdocuments.gov.
91 "Miss Anthony knew" Catt, *Woman Suffrage*, digital.
91 "The right" Oregonian, June 23, 1873.
91 "The right of voting" Ibid.
91 "There was" Carrie Catt, *Woman Suffrage*, 1923, digital ed.
91 "Has the" Doris Stevens, *Jailed for Freedom*, 1921, digital ed.
91 "Yes, your Honor" Ibid.
91 "Robbed of the" Ibid.
92 "The court cannot" Ibid.
92 "May it please" Ibid.
92 "The court cannot" Ibid.
92 "But, your Honor" Ibid.
92 "The prisoner" Ibid.
92 "Of all my persecutors" Ibid.
92 "The court must insist" Ibid.
93 "Yes, your Honor" Ibid.
93 "The court orders" Ibid.
93 "When I was" Ibid.
93 "The sentence of" Ibid
93 "May it please your Honor" Ibid.
93 "Madam, the court" Ibid.
94 "She was a shrewd" Ibid.

Chapter 6: Switching Tactics
Page #
94 "Susan B. Anthony's" *New York Herald*, Nov. 16, 1872.
94 "The delegates to" *Kalamazoo Gazette*, March 8, 1884.
94 "The president stood" Ibid.
95 "The president was" Ibid.
95 "This answer did" Ibid.
95 "Miss Anthony, we would" Ibid.
95 "A polygamous" *Daily Critic*, March 10, 1884.
95 "Susan B. Anthony and Delegate Caine" Ibid.
95 "Miss Anthony took" Ibid.
95 "Mr. Caine argued" Ibid.
95 "Susan B. Anthony has been" *The Sun*, (C.O.) March 15, 1884.
96 "And without giving" Ibid.
96 "Miss Anthony and" Evening Star, (D.C) March 8, 1884
96 "After concluding their" Ibid.
96 "When, however, she" Ibid.
97 "Dear Mr." Ida Harper, *Life Work Susan B. Anthony*, 1899, digital ed.
97 "I realize that at" Ibid.
98 "It would be as noble" Ibid.

98 "So long as you" Doris Stevens, *Jailed for Freedom*, 1921, digital ed.
98 "If all the suffragists" Ibid.
98 "Until that good" Ibid.
102 "The salvation of the" Ibid.

Chapter 7: Perseverance on a Spring
Page #
101 "While women" *Columbia Herald*, Dec. 23, 1892.
102 "for the public" Ibid.
102 "Like all martyrs" Ibid.
103 "Speaking at" *Washington Bee*, Oct. 29, 1892.
103 "All eyes" Ibid.
103 "All eyes" Ibid.
103 "As a platform" Ibid.
103 "In a public" Ibid.
104 "In her lecture" Ibid.
104 "At the testimonial" Ibid.
104 "Speaking at" *Afro-American Advocate*, June 30, 1893.
104 "How enfranchisement" *Original Rights*, June 1910.
105 "The flower" Ibid.
105 "an absolute dead" Ibid.
105 "persons of" Ibid.
105 "The right of citizens" Ibid.
105 "These rights" Ibid.
106 "With no sacredness" Ibid.
106 "The mob says" Ibid.
106 "Therefore the more" Ibid.
107 "It is believed" Ibid.
107 "Harvard bars suffragette" *Elkhart Daily Review*, Oct. 23, 1909.
107 "Miss Milholland" Ibid.
108 "One of her" *Daily Alaska Dispatch*, Nov. 28, 1916.
108 "Inez Milholland" *New York Sun*, Dec. 4, 1909.
108 "Since the shirtwaist" Ibid.
109 "Every principal" *Salt Lake Telegram*, March 3, 1913.
109 "That is what" Ibid.
109 "Washington, March 3" Ibid.
109 "This is an age" Ibid.
110 "This is what" Ibid.
110 "It will present" Ibid.
110 "Realizing the value" Ibid.
110 "When men see" Ibid.
111 "The awakened" Ibid.
111 "The thinking" Ibid.

111 "As men know" Ibid.

111 "And men are" Ibid.

Chapter 8: Resilience on Parade

Page #

116 "Miss Inez" *Colorado Springs Gazette*, March 4, 1913.

116 "Miss Milholland" Ibid.

117 "A tall man" *Denver Post*, March 4, 1913.

117 "Miss Inez Milholland, wearing" Ibid.

117 "Her hair falling" Ibid.

117 "attired as" *Daily Advocate,* Stamford, CT, March 3, 1913

117 "the crusade" Ibid.

117 "We demand" *Washington Herald*, March 4, 1913.

118 "Man and woman" Ibid.

118 "We prepare our" Ibid.

118 "Word had gone" Ibid.

118 "When the mice" Ibid.

118 "If anyone lets" Ibid.

119 "Growing impatient" *Denver Post*, March 4, 1913.

119 "At a cross" Ibid.

119 "You men should" Ibid.

119 "fell back respectfully" Ibid.

119 "Mizz Inez Milholland" Ibid.

119 "Inez Milholland" *Cleburne Morning Review*, TX March 4, 1913.

119 "rode up beside" Ibid.

120 "Women in big pageant" *Washington Herald*, March 4, 1913.

120 "Inez Milholland on" Ibid.

120 "Suffragists insulted" *Denver Post*, March 4, 1913.

120 "a mob of hooting" Ibid.

120 "Women have free" *Washington Herald*, March 4, 1913.

120 "instance of a hoodlum" *Denver Post*, March 4, 1913.

120 "a ruffian broke" Ibid.

120 "The girls carrying" Ibid.

120 "Angry women" Ibid.

120 "A group of hoodlums" Ibid.

121 "defies sentiment" *Washington Herald*, March 4, 1913.

121 "Mrs. Ida Wells-Barnett" Ibid.

121 "Nine states" *Denver Post*, March 4, 1913.

121 "But some of" *Washington Herald*, March 4, 1913.

121 "Wherefore Mrs. Barnett" Ibid.

122 "But the Illinois" Ibid.

122 "and I shall" Ibid.

122 "Mrs. Barnett not only" *Cleveland Gazette*, March 15, 1913.

122 "It might be" *Broad Ax*, March 8, 1913.

122 "to represent the" *Broad Ax,* Nov. 15, 1913.

122 "to get hold" Ibid.

123 "It was a day of" *Washington Herald*, March 4, 1913.

123 "A German submarine" *Trenton Evening Times*, June 2, 1915.

123 "Most beautiful suffragette" Ibid.

124 "I have this" Ibid.

124 "As we approached" Ibid.

124 "Mrs. Eugene Boissevain" *Tulsa World*, Aug. 31, 1915.

124 "The Italian authorities" Ibid.

125 "The unenfranchised," "Milholand Speech," *Suffragist*, Oct. 14, 1916

125 "The dominant" Ibid.

126 "They have blocked" Ibid.

126 "Therefore, women" Ibid.

126 "Now, for the first" Ibid.

126 "Women of the West" Ibid.

126 "Liberty must" Ibid.

127 "Sister of the West" Ibid.

127 "Women of the West, stand" Ibid.

127 "The gods of" Ibid.

127 "Most beautiful" *Topeka Journal*, Oct. 2, 1916.

127 "Miss Milholland" Ibid.

127 "Say to the, stand," "Millholand Speech," *Suffragist*, Oct. 14, 1916.

128 "We, as women" Ibid.

128 "Mrs. Boissevan?" *Evening Star*, D.C. Nov. 27, 1916.

128 "We have no" Ibid.

128 "Here and there" Ibid.

129 "Women of these" Ibid.

129 "It is only" Ibid.

129 "Noted suffrage" *Evening Star*, D.C. Nov. 27, 1916.

129 "Mrs. Inez" Ibid.

129 "In 8 years" *Trenton Evening Times*, Nov. 27, 1916.

129 "Perhaps there never" Ibid.

129 "Mrs. Boissevain" *Evening Star*, D.C. Nov. 27, 1916.

129 "It is a loss" Ibid.

Chapter 9: Courageous Creativity
Page #

133 "Lucy Burns the suffragist" *Oregonian*, Oct. 8, 1916.

133 "the height" Inez Gillmore, *Story of the Woman's Party*, 1921, 154.

134 "The flight was" *Oregonian*, Oct. 8, 1916.

134 "President Wilson's" *Aberdeen American*, Dec. 6, 1916.

134 "Suffrage banner" Ibid.

135 "He was just" Ibid.
135 "As the banner" Ibid.
135 "The president" Ibid.
135 "Miss Lucy Burns" Ibid.
135 "When he finished" Ibid.
135 "We feel did" Ibid.
136 "The death" Doris Stevens, *Jailed for Freedom*, 1921, digital ed.
136 "We ask you" Ibid.
136 "It is impossible" Ibid.
137 "They are not" Ibid.
137 "We have gone" Ibid.
137 "Yet he tells" Ibid.
137 "Yet he is" Ibid.
137 "We have to" Ibid.
138 "We have got" Ibid.
138 "Won't you" Ibid.
138 "heroically sculptured" Ibid.
138 "It fell to Lucy Burns" Ibid.
138 "If particular care" Abigail Adams to John Adams, March 31, 1776.
139 "has a mental poise" Ibid.
139 "Women are after" *Daily Alaska Dispatch*, AK, Jan. 10, 1917.
139 "The women's suffrage" Ibid.
139 "Mr. President" Ibid.
139 "White House officials" *Cleveland Plain Dealer*, OH, Jan. 11, 1917.
139 "Suffrage pickets" Ibid.
140 "The White House police" Ibid.
140 "The announced purpose" Ibid.
140 "we demand " Doris Stevens, *Jailed for Freedom*, 1921, digital ed.
141 "Cries of 'traitor'" *Olympia Daily Recorder*, June 20, 1917.
141 "You are a dirty" *Topeka State Journal*, June 21, 1917.
141 "Banners of Silent" *Olympia Daily Recorder*, June 20, 1917.
141 "Bearing their" *Sun and New York Press*, June 21, 1917.
141 "To the Russian" Doris Stevens, *Jailed for Freedom*, 1921, digital ed.
142 "We the women" Ibid.
142 "Help us make" Ibid.
142 "It's an outrage" *Sun and New York Press*, June 21, 1917.
142 "Miss Burns" Ibid.
142 "The police obtained" Ibid.
142 "The two banner" Ibid.
143 "The National Woman's Party" Ibid.
143 "Dr. Anna Howard Shaw" Ibid.
143 "that the president" *Sun and New York Press*, June 21, 1917.
144 "For the President" Doris Stevens, *Jailed for Freedom*, 1921, digital ed.

144 "Nevertheless, we are" Ibid.

144 "We shall fight" Ibid.

145 "Governments derive" Ibid.

145 "The manhandling" Ibid.

146 "If the situation" Ibid.

146 "that although we" Ibid.

146 "The enfranshisement" Ibid.

146 "Mr. President" Ibid.

147 "Shoot at suffs" *Trenton Evening Times*, Aug. 15, 1917.

147 "For two hours" Ibid.

147 "Kaiser Wilson" Doris Stevens, *Jailed for Freedom*, 1921, digital ed.

147 "Miss Lucy Burns" *Trenton Evening Times*, Aug. 15, 1917.

148 "But for Miss" Doris Stevens, *Jailed for Freedom*, 1921, digital ed.

148 "striking at the" *Trenton Evening Times*, Aug. 15, 1917.

148 "shower of missiles" Ibid.

148 "Why did you" Ibid.

148 "A sailor with" Ibid.

148 "The most moving" Peggy Noonan, *On Speaking Well*, 1999.

148 "It's the logic" Ibid.

149 "It shows respect" Ibid.

149 "Lucy Burns'" *Daily Gate City*, Aug. 24, 1917.

149 "That restless egotist" Ibid.

150 "In her 'Kaiser Wilson" Ibid.

150 "Thus there is" Ibid.

150 "Even picketing" Ibid.

150 "All is well" Ibid.

150 "Yet the sinister" Ibid.

151 "We have been" Doris Stevens, *Jailed for Freedom*, digital.

152 "We have fogotten" Ibid.

152 "Mr. President" *Denver Rocky Mountain News*, Aug. 18, 1917

152 "The government" Ibid.

152 "50 arrested" *Wilkes-Barre Times Leader*, Aug. 29, 1917.

152 "Her convictions" Doris Stevens, *Jailed for Freedom*, digital.

Chapter 10: Creative Courage & the Night of Terror
Page #

157 "When our friends" Doris Stevens, 1921, *Jailed for Freedom*.

157 "The hominy" Evening Capital, Nov. 27, 1917.

157 "The hygenic" Doris Stevens, *Jailed for Freedom*, 1921, digital ed.

158 "The same piece" Ibid.

158 "Concerning the" Ibid.

158 "The prisoners for" Ibid.

159 "Mr. President" Ibid.

159 "Dudley F. Malone" *Pueblo Chieftain*, Sept. 8, 1917.

159 "Malone resigns" *Butte Daily Post*, Sept. 7, 1917.

159 "Malone quits" *Aberdeen American*, Sept. 8, 1917.

160 "Protest to Wilson" *Pueblo Chieftain*, Sept. 8, 1917.

160 "Dudley Field Malone" *Aberdeen American*, Sept. 8, 1917.

160 "felt obliged" Ibid.

160 "Last autumn" Ibid.

160 "The most difficult" Ibid.

160 "rest of those" Ibid.

161 "And if the women" Ibid.

161 "But the present" Ibid.

161 "And if the men" Ibid.

161 "To me, Mr. President" Ibid.

161 "But unless the" Doris Stevens, *Jailed for Freedom*, 1921, digital ed.

162 "For this reason" Ibid.

162 "It is true" *Aberdeen American*, Sept. 8, 1917.

162 "For the whole" Doris Stevens, *Jailed for Freedom*, 1921, digital ed.

163 "As political" Evening Star, D.C. Oct. 19, 1917.

163 "We have taken" Ibid.

163 "Conscious therefore" Ibid.

163 "We ask exemption" Ibid.

163 "Miss Lucy Burns" Ibid.

164 "Militant suffs now" *Sun and New York Press*, Nov. 14, 1917.

164 "White House picketer" Ibid.

164 "Scene House" Ibid.

164 "Whereupon there" Ibid.

164 "That is what" Ibid.

165 "New York has" *Wilkes-Barre Times Leader*, Nov. 7, 1917.

164 "There is" Ibid.

165 "Twelve thousand" Ibid.

165 "The feared negative" Ibid.

165 "President Wilson's support" Ibid.

165 "Wilson gives full" *Cleveland Plain Dealer*, Oct. 26, 1917.

165 "the president" *Wilkes-Barre Times Leader*, Nov. 7, 1917.

165 "admitted that" *Sun and New York Press*, Nov. 14, 1917.

166 "Miss Lucy" *Denver Rocky Mountain News*, Nov. 15, 1917.

166 "Miss Lucy Burns denounced" Ibid.

166 "Your honor" Ibid.

166 "You are a menace" Ibid.

166 "I wouldn't" Ibid.

166 "I wouldn't" *Sun and New York Press*, Nov. 17, 1917.

166 "Organization plans" Ibid.

167 "Occoquan guard" *Denver Post*, Nov. 17, 1917.

167 "threatens to" Ibid.
167 "Story of" *Sun and New York Press*, Nov. 17, 1917.
167 "Washington November 17" Ibid.
167 "Washington November 14" Ibid.
167 "Seized by guards" Ibid.
168 "I was handcuffed" Ibid.
168 "Thursday, November 16" Ibid.
168 "Thirty suffragists" *Colorado Springs Gazette*, Nov. 18, 1917.
169 "In the name" *Sun and New York Press*, Nov. 17, 1917.
169 "I saw aone" Doris Stevens, *Jailed for Freedom*, 1921, digital ed.
169 "I was trembling" Ibid.
169 "I . . . saw the guards" Ibid.
169 "The whole group" Ibid.
169 "There was no" Ibid.
170 "Furthermore the water" Ibid.
170 "Stop that" Ibid.
170 "I was exhausted" Ibid.
170 "It seemed to" Ibid.
170 "It is impossible" Ibid.
170 "twenty-two pickets" *Dallas Morning News*, Nov. 28, 1917.
171 "Woman's party" Ibid.
171 "Wilson comes out" *Pueblo Chieftan*, Jan. 10, 1918.
171 "The committee found" Ibid.
171 "The Susan B. Anthony" *Broad Ax*, Jan. 12, 1918.
172 "The amendment now" Ibid.
172 "I regard the" Doris Stevens, *Jailed for Freedom*, 1921, digital ed.
172 "Are we alone" Ibid.
172 "His speech eloquent" Ibid.
173 "What should we" Ibid.
173 "Women Win in" *Jackson City Patriot*, June 5, 1919.
174 "Amendment wins" *Oregonian*, June 5, 1919.
174 "Suffrage Now" *The Sun*, June 5, 1919.

Chapter 11: Remembering a Lady
Page #
177 "They were both" Tyler Boyd, *Tennessee Statesman*, 2019, digital ed.
177 "Strong opposition" Ibid.
177 "Ninety percent" Ibid.
177 "A vote for" Ibid.
177 "to agitate" Ibid.
178 "I don't like" Ibid.
178 "an old woman" Ibid.
179 "If there is anything" Ibid.

180 "beautifully organized" Ibid.
180 "baited with whiskey" Ibid.
180 "I cannot pledge" Ibid.
180 "The majority" Ibid.
181 "I tell you" Ibid.
181 "Vote on suffrage" *Times-Picayune*, Aug. 17, 1920.
181 "Tennessee leaders" Ibid.
181 "Seth Walker" Ibid.
181 "As he walked" Tyler Boyd, *Tennessee Statesman*, 2019, digital ed.
182 "We really" Ibid.
182 "The gallery of the" Ibid.
182 "Nothing as big" Ibid.
182 "Believing the amendment" Ibid.
182 "The roll call began" Ibid.
183 "Aye, Burn said quickly" Ibid.
183 "It was pendemonium" Ibid.
184 "I just stepped" Ibid.
184 "So, I just alked" Ibid.
184 "But I outran them" Ibid.
185 "No human being" Ibid.
185 "Youngest member" *Seattle Daily Times*, Aug. 20, 1920.
185 "Terrible pressure" *Chattanooga News*, TN, Aug. 20, 1920.
185 "Harry, I've known" Ibid.
185 "You can't make" Ibid.
185 "Harry that was" *Tyler Boyd, Tennessee Statesman*, 2019, digital ed.
186 "I desire" Ibid.
186 "And it is my" Ibid.
186 "I know they" Ibid.
186 "First I believe" *Chattanooga News*, Aug. 19, 1920.
186 "Third I know" Ibid.
186 "Fourth, I appreciated" Ibid.
187 "Followed his mother's" *Seattle Daily Times*, Aug. 20, 1920.
187 "Mother proud" *New York Daily Tribune*, Aug. 21, 1920.
187 "I am glad he" Ibid.
187 "The first news" Ibid.
187 "Hurrah, and" Tyler Boyd, *Tennessee Statesman*, 2019, digital ed.
187 "But I do hope" Ibid.
187 "Don't forget to" Ibid.
188 "In regard to" *Chattanooga News*, Aug. 20, 1920.
188 "I believe it is" *New York Daily Tribune*, Aug. 21, 1920.
188 "But I did know" Ibid.
189 "I have hired" Ibid.
189 "I think suffrage" Ibid.

189 "Had more" Carrie Catt, *Woman Suffrage*, 1923, digital ed.
190 "the deflecting" Ibid.
190 "But when the" Ibid.

Suffragists at the White House, (Library of Congress)

BIBLIOGRAPHY

"22 Woman's Party Hunger Strikers Released from Jail," *Dallas Morning News*, Nov. 28, 1917, https://www.genealogybank.com (accessed Feb. 4, 2020).

"30 Pickets Sentenced to 30 Days in Occoquan," *Denver Rocky Mountain News*, Nov. 15, 1917, https://www.genealogybank.com/ accessed Feb. 4, 2020.

"A Colored Courday," *Columbia Herald* (TN), Dec. 23, 1892, https://www.genealogybank.com/ (accessed Feb. 4, 2020).

"A Polygamous Discussion," *Daily Critic, (D.C.)*, March 10, 1884, https://www.genealogybank.com/ (accessed Feb. 4, 2020).

"American Equal Rights Association," *New York Herald*, July 5, 1867, https://www.genealogybank.com/ (accessed Feb. 4, 2020).

"Banners of Silent Sentinels before White House Torn down by Angry Mob," *Olympia Daily Recorder, (WA)*, June 20, 1917, https://www.genealogybank.com/ (accessed Feb. 4, 2020).

"Big Pageant is Unprotected," *Washington Herald, (D.C.)* March 4, 1913, ps://www.genealogybank.com/ (accessed Feb. 4, 2020).

"Burns' Vote Was Influence by His Mother's Views," *Chattanooga News*, Aug. 19, 1920, https://www.genealogybank.com/ (accessed Feb. 4, 2020).

"Candler Says Charges Against Burn Are Too Ridiculous," *Chattanooga News*, Aug. 20, 1920, https://www.genealogybank.com/ (accessed Feb. 4, 2020).

"Colorado Women Protest To Capital," *Colorado Springs Gazette*, Nov. 18, 1917, https://www.genealogybank.com (accessed Feb. 4, 2020).

"Compare the Two Speeches" https://www.thesojournertruthproject.com/compare-the-speeches/ accessed Feb. 4, 2020.

"Death Overtakes Inez Boissevain," *Trenton Evening Times*, Trenton, New Jersey, Nov. 27, 1916, https://www.genealogybank.com/ (accessed Feb. 4, 2020).

"Declaration of Independence," National Archives, July 4, 1776, https://www.archives.gov/founding-docs/declaration (accessed Feb. 4, 2020).

"Declaration of Sentiments," *The Liberator, (MA)*, Aug. 25, 1848, http://www.Genealogybank.com (accessed Nov. 9, 2019).

"Doings of the Race," *Cleveland Gazette*, March 15, 1913, ps://www.genealogybank.com/ (accessed Feb. 4, 2020).

"Dudley F, Malone Resigns as Custom Collector at N. Y. Protests to Wilson Against Failure of President to Support Suffrage Amendment," *Pueblo Chieftain*, *(CO)*, Sept. 8, 1917, https://www.genealogybank.com/ (accessed Feb. 4, 2020).

"Every Principle, However Splendid, Needs Advocating, Declares Miss Milholland" *Salt Lake Telegram*, March 3, 1913, https://www.genealogybank.com/ (accessed Feb. 4, 2020).

"First Women's Rights Movement" Ohio History Connection, https://ohiohistorycentral.org/w/First_Women%27s_Rights_Moveme nt (accessed Feb. 4, 2020).

"Followed His Mother's Advice," *Seattle Daily Times*, Seattle, Aug. 20, 1920, https://www.genealogybank.com/ (accessed Feb. 4, 2020).

"Former Inez Milholland Goes to Italian Army," *Tulsa World*, Aug. 31, 1915, https://www.genealogybank.com/ (accessed Feb. 4, 2020).

"Harvard bars suffragette," *Elkhart Daily Review*, Oct. 23, 1909, https://www.genealogybank.com/ (accessed Feb. 4, 2020).

"How Enfranchisement Stops Lynching," *Original Rights,* (NY), June 1910.

"Inez Milholland on White Horse Charges Street Mob," *Cleburne Morning Review*, (TX), March 4, 1913, https://www.genealogybank.com/ (accessed Feb. 4, 2020).

"Jefferson's 'original Rough draught' of the Declaration of Independence" Library of Congress, https://www.loc.gov/exhibits/declara/ruffdrft.html (accessed Feb. 4, 2020).

"Lucy Burns Made Fast to the Bars, She Says" *Sun and New York Press*, Nov. 17, 1917, https://www.genealogybank.com/ (accessed Feb. 4, 2020).

"Lucy Burns' Battalion of Death," *Daily Gate City and Constitution Democrat*, (IO), Aug. 24, 1917, https://www.genealogybank.com (accessed Feb. 4, 2020).

"Malone Quits as a Protest Against Arrest of Suffs Customs Collector at New York Tenders," *Aberdeen American*, *(SD)*, Sept. 8, 1917, https://www.genealogybank.com/ accessed (Feb. 4, 2020).

"Militant Suffs Will Nominate 2 for Congress," *Sun and New York Press*, Nov. 14, 1917, https://www.genealogybank.com/ (accessed Feb. 4, 2020).

"Miss Ida Wells England," *Afro-American Advocate*, Coffeyville, Kansas June

30, 1893, https://www.genealogybank.com/ (accessed Feb. 4, 2020).

"Miss Inez Milholland," *Colorado Springs Gazette*, March 4, 1913, https://www.genealogybank.com/ (accessed Feb. 4, 2020).

"Miss Susan B. Anthony and a Delegation," *Evening Star*, (D.C.), March 8, 1884, https://www.genealogybank.com (accessed Feb. 4, 2020).

"More Women's Rights Conventions," National Parks Service, https://www.nps.gov/wori/learn/historyculture/more-womens-rights-conventions.htm (accessed Feb. 4, 2020).

"Most Beautiful Suffragette" *Trenton Evening Times*, June 2, 1915, https://www.genealogybank.com/ (accessed Feb. 4, 2020).

"Mother Proud of Son Who Cast Deciding Vote for Suffrage," *New York Daily Tribune*, Aug. 21, 1920, https://www.genealogybank.com/ (accessed Feb. 4, 2020).

"Mrs. Catt Opposes Heckling Methods," *Arkansas Gazette*, June 22, 1917, https://www.genealogybank.com/ (accessed Feb. 4, 2020).

"Noted Suffrage Worker Is Dead," *Evening Star*, (D.C.), Nov. 27, 1916, https://www.genealogybank.com (accessed Feb. 4, 2020).

"Occoquan Guard Accused by Suffragists," *Denver Post*, Nov. 17, 1917, https://www.genealogybank.com/ (accessed Feb. 4, 2020).

"Paraders is Censured by All," *Denver Post*, March 4, 1913, https://www.genealogybank.com/ (accessed Feb. 4, 2020).

"Pickets on Strike Decline to Work," *Evening Star*, (D.C.), Oct. 19, 1917, https://www.genealogybank.com/ (accessed Feb. 4, 2020).

"President's Address Marked by Suffrage," *Aberdeen American*, (SD), Dec. 6, 1916, https://www.genealogybank.com/ (accessed Feb. 4, 2020).

"Righteousness Exhalteth a Nation," *Washington Bee*, Oct. 29, 1892, https://www.genealogybank.com/ (accessed Feb. 4, 2020).

"Senate Passes Suffrage Bill Amendment Now Goes to the States for Ratification. Vote is 56," *Baltimore Sun*, (MD), June 5, 1919, https://www.genealogybank.com/ (accessed Feb. 4, 2020).

"She Comes Here" *Topeka Journal*, Oct. 2, 1916, https://www.genealogybank.com/ (accessed Feb. 4, 2020).

"Shoot at Suffs," *Trenton Evening Times*, Aug. 15, 191, https://www.genealogybank.com (accessed Feb. 4, 2020).

"Six Suffrage Pickets Jailes," *Denver Rocky Mountain News*, Aug. 18, 1917, https://www.genealogybank.com (accessed Feb. 4, 2020).

"Sojourner Truth" National Parks Service,
https://www.nps.gov/wori/learn/historyculture/sojourner-truth.htm
(accessed Feb. 4, 2020).

"Stormy Career of Suffragist," *Daily Alaska Dispatch*, Nov. 28, 1916,
https://www.genealogybank.com/ (accessed Feb. 4, 2020).

"Suffrage Adopted in Senate 56 to 25," *Oregonian*, June 5, 1919,
https://www.genealogybank.com/ (accessed Feb. 4, 2020).

"Suffrage Pickets Flaunt Banners At White House Congressional Union
Members Hold Silent Vigil Before Gates," *Cleveland Plain Dealer*, Jan. 11,
1917, https://www.genealogybank.com/ (accessed Feb. 4, 2020).

"Suffrage Pickets Gain Hostility of Co-Workers," *Wilkes-Barre Times Leader*,
(PA), Aug. 29, 1917, https://www.genealogybank.com (accessed Feb.
4, 2020).

"Suffrage Wins By 274 To 136," *Broad Ax*, (IL), Jan. 12, 1918,
https://www.genealogybank.com/ (accessed Feb. 4, 2020).

"Suffragist Writes Prison Conditions," *Evening Capital and Maryland Gazette*,
Nov. 27, 1917, https://www.genealogybank.com/ (accessed Feb. 4,
2020).

"Suffragists Insulted by Rowdies in Crowd," *Denver Post*, (CO) March 4,
1913, https://www.genealogybank.com/ (accessed Feb. 4, 2020).

"Susan B," *The Sun*, (CO), March 15, 1884,
https://www.genealogybank.com/ (accessed Feb. 4, 2020).

"Susan B. Anthony in trouble," *New York Herald*, Nov. 16, 1872,
https://www.genealogybank.com/ (accessed Feb. 4, 2020).

"Susan B. Anthony, Uncle Sam" *Pomeroy's Democrat*, (NY), Jan. 25, 1873,
https://www.genealogybank.com/ (accessed Feb. 4, 2020).

"Susan B. Anthony," *Daily Illinois State Register*, March 30, 1884,
https://www.genealogybank.com/ (accessed Feb. 4, 2020).

"The Alpha Suffrage Club to Give a Banquet," *Broad Ax*, (IL), Nov. 15,
1913, https://www.genealogybank.com/ (accessed Feb. 4, 2020).

"The Anniversaries. American Equal Rights Association," *Evening Post*,
New York, May 15, 1868, p. 2. https://www.genealogybank.com/
accessed Feb. 4, 2020.

"The Equal Suffrage Parade was Viewed by Many Thousand People,"
Broad Ax, (IL), March 8, 1913, ps://www.genealogybank.com/
(accessed Feb. 4, 2020).

"The Office Malone Gives Up," *Butte Daily Post*, (MT), Sept. 7, 1917, https://www.genealogybank.com/ (accessed Feb. 4, 2020).

"The President and the Suffragists," *Kalamazoo Gazette*, March 8, 1884, https://www.genealogybank.com/ (accessed Feb. 4, 2020).

"The Susan B. Anthony Case," *Public Ledger*, (*PA*), December 27, 1872, https://www.genealogybank.com/ (accessed Feb. 4, 2020).

"Trial of Susan B. Anthony," *Oregonian*, June 23, 1873.

"Vote On Suffrage To Be Close, Say 'Pros' And 'Antis' Tennessee Leaders of Both Sides," *Times-Picayune*, (*LA*), Aug. 17, 1920, https://www.genealogybank.com/ (accessed Feb. 4, 2020).

"What Women Voters Want," *New York Sun*, Dec. 4, 1909, https://www.genealogybank.com/ (accessed Feb. 4, 2020).

"Wilson and Root Assailed," *Sun and New York Press*, June 21, 1917, https://www.genealogybank.com/ (accessed Feb. 4, 2020).

"Wilson Comes Out for Suffrage," *Pueblo Chieftan*, (*CO*), Jan. 10, 1918, https://www.genealogybank.com (accessed Feb. 4, 2020).

"Wilson Gives Full Support To Suffrage," *Cleveland Plain Dealer*, Oct. 26, 1917, https://www.genealogybank.com (accessed Feb. 4, 2020).

"Woman Suffrage Win in New York," *Wilkes-Barre Times Leader*, (*PA*), Nov. 7, 1917, https://www.genealogybank.com (accessed Feb. 4, 2020).

"Woman's Rights Convention," *Evening Star*, (*NY*), Oct. 21, 1854, https://www.genealogybank.com/ (accessed Feb. 4, 2020).

"Woman's Rights Convention. Speeches by Lucy Stone, Wm. Lloyd Garrison, Lucretia Mott and Others," *Evening Post*, (*NY*), Oct. 19, 1854, https://www.genealogybank.com/ (accessed Feb. 4, 2020).

"Woman's Rights Eleventh National Convention of the Strong Minded Females," *New York Herald*, May 11, 1866, https://www.genealogybank.com/ (accessed Feb. 4, 2020).

"Women Are after Wilson for Suffrage Woman Suffragette after Another Futile Appeal to President Are Preparing for Demonstration," *Daily Alaska Dispatch*, Jan. 10, 1917, https://www.genealogybank.com/ (accessed Feb. 4, 2020).

"Women Fight, Weep and Rip Suff Banners," *Topeka State Journal*, June 21, 1917, https://www.genealogybank.com/ (accessed Feb. 4, 2020).

"Women Win In Senate; Fight Goes To States," *Jackson City Patriot*, (*MI*), June 5, 1919, https://www.genealogybank.com/ (accessed Feb. 4, 2020).

"Wonders in Many Lands," *Oregonian*, Oct. 8, 1916, https://www.genealogybank.com/ (accessed Feb. 4, 2020).

Fourteenth Amendment Transcription, Our Documents, http://www.ourdocuments.gov/doc.php?flash=false&doc=43&page=transcript (accessed Feb. 4, 2020).

Fifteenth Amendment Transcription, Our Documents, http://www.ourdocuments.gov/doc.php?flash=false&doc=43&page=transcript (accessed Feb. 4, 2020).

Adams, Abigail. *To John Adams*, Dec. 10, 1775, Feb. 21, 1776, March 2, 1776, March 31, 1776, July 3, 1776, http://Founders.archives.gov (accessed Feb. 4, 2020).

_____. *To Edward Dilly*, May 22, 1775, http://Founders.archives.gov, (accessed Feb. 4, 2020).

Adams, John. *To Abigail Adams*, Dec. 3, 1775, Feb. 16, 1776, March 19, 1776, April 14, 177, April 28, 1776, May 17, 1776, May 22, 1776, May 27, 1776, http://Founders.archives.gov (accessed, Feb. 4, 2020).

_____. *To Hezekiah Niles*, Feb. 13, 1818, http://Founders.archives.gov (accessed Feb. 4, 2020).

_____. *To James Sullivan*, May 26, 1776, http://Founders.archives.gov (accessed Feb. 4, 2020).

Allen, Orrin Peer. *Descendants of Nicholas Cady of Watertown, Mass. 1645-1910*. Palmer: Press of C.B. Fiske & Company, 1910.

Boissevain, Inez Milholland. "Inez Milholland Speech." *The Suffragist*. Oct. 14, 1916.

Boyd, Tyler L. *Tennessee Statesman Harry T. Burn: Woman Suffrage, Free Elections & a Life of Service*. Charleston: The History Press, 2019.

Catt, Carrie Chapman and Shuler, Nettie Rogers. *Woman Suffrage and Politics: The Inner Story of the Suffrage Movement*. New York: Charles Scribner's Sons, 1923, digital edition accessed Feb. 4, 2020.

Coates, Steve. "Abraham Lincoln and Sojourner Truth." *New York Times*. Oct. 29, 2010. https://artsbeat.blogs.nytimes.com/2010/10/29/abraham-lincoln-and-sojourner-truth/ (accessed Feb. 4, 2020).

Gillmore, Inez Haynes. *The Story of the Woman's Party*. New York: Harcourt Brace, 1921.

Harper, Ida Husted. *Life and Work of Susan B. Anthony*. Indianapolis and Kansas City: Bowen-Merrill Company, 1899.

Locke, John. *Two Treatises of Government.* London: Black Swan by Amen-Corner London, 1690. Digital edition accessed Feb. 4, 2020.

Mott, Lucretia. *Discourse on Women.* Speech, Assembly Buildings. Dec. 17, 1849. Philadelphia: T.B. Peterson, 1850.

Noonan, Peggy. *On Speaking Well: How to Give a Speech with Style, Substance, and Clarity.* New York: William Morrow, 1999.

Paine, Thomas. *Common Sense: Addressed to the Inhabitants of America.* Philadelphia, 1776.

Ratcliffe, Donald. "The Right to Vote and the Rise of Democracy, 1787-1828." *Journal of the Early Republic* 33, No. 2 (Summer 2013). 219-254.

Robinson, Marius. "On Woman's Right." *Anti-Slavery Bugle* (OH). June 21, 1851.

Shaw, Elizabeth Smith. *To Abigail Adams*, Dec. 29, 1793.

Sklar, Kathryn Kish. "The Schooling of Girls and Changing Community Values in Massachusetts Towns, 1750-1820." *History of Education Quarterly* 33, No. 4 (1993). 511-542.

Stanton, Elizabeth Cady. *Eighty Years and More: (1815-1897) Reminiscences of Elizabeth Cady Stanton.* New York: European Publishing Company, 1898.

Steinfeld, Robert J. "Property and Suffrage in the Early American Republic." *Stanford Law Review* 41, No. 2 (1989). 335-376. doi:10.2307/1228746.

Stevens, Doris. *Jailed for Freedom.* New York: Boni and Liveright, 1920, digital edition accessed in 2020.

Sullivan, James. *To Elbridge Gerry.* May 17, 1776, Founders.archives.gov (accessed Feb. 4, 2020)

Truth, Sojourner. *Narrative of Sojourner Truth.* Boston: J.B. Yerrington and Sons, 1850. https://docsouth.unc.edu/neh/truth50/truth50.html

U.S. Constitution. National Archives. www.Nara.gov. (accessed Feb. 4, 2020)

America, 1870 (Library of Congress)

Statue of Liberty, for the freedom of the world, 1917
(Library of Congress)

Votes for Women Billboard, (Library of Congress)

Suffragists in New Jersey hanging signs on the boardwalk
(Library of Congress)

Votes for Women, (Library of Congress)

ABOUT THE AUTHOR

Jane Hampton Cook is an award-winning screenwriter and author of ten books, a national media commentator, and former White House webmaster to President George W. Bush. A contributor to TheHill.com and GenealogyBank.com, Jane is a frequent guest on the Fox News Channel, CNN, BBC, SKY News, CNBC, and other media outlets. She was a historical consultant for the Women's Suffrage Centennial Commission in 2019-20. An on-camera storyteller and cast member, Jane has appeared on Brian Kilmeade's WHAT MADE AMERICA GREAT? on Fox Nation to discuss this book, the George Washington documentary THE FIRST AMERICAN, and the History Channel's UNITED STUFF OF AMERICA.

Inspired by her 9/11 evacuation from the White House, her feature screenplay SAVING WASHINGTON placed third out of 1,000 entries in ScreenCraft's 2018 drama screenwriting contest. SAVING WASHINGTON is adapted from her book, The Burning of the White House: James and Dolley Madison and the War of 1812. Jane received a bachelor's degree from Baylor University, a master's degree from Texas A&M University, and a research fellowship from the Organization of American Historians and White House Historical Association. She currently lives with her husband and their children in a Washington, D.C., suburb. www.janecook.com.

Jane Hampton Cook's Books

*The Burning of the White House: James & Dolley Madison
& the War of 1812*

*American Phoenix: John Quincy & Louisa Adams, the War of 1812
& the Exile that Saved American Independence*

America's Star-Spangled Story

Stories of Faith & Courage from the War in Iraq & Afghanistan

Stories of Faith and Courage from the Revolutionary War

The Faith of America's First Ladies

For Children
*What Does the President Look Like?
B is for Baylor
Maggie Houston*

Made in the USA
Monee, IL
25 February 2021